The Long White

Cloud of Unknowing

The Long

White Cloud

of Unknowing

Lisa Samuels

chax 2019

ISBN 978-1-946104-18-2
Library of Congress Control Number: 2019943662

Chax Press
1517 N Wilmot Rd no. 264
Tucson Arizona 85712-4410

Chax Press books are supported in part by individual donors, by sales of the books, and, from 2015-2019, by a fund at the University of Houston-Victoria. Please visit *https://chax.org/membership-support/* if you would like to contribute to our mission to make an impact on the literature and culture of our time.

Chax Press intern Katie Ray provided essential assistance, in design, layout, proofreading, and on other aspects of this book.

Acknowledgments:

Cover image, *Sala 12,* from *Retablos Contemporáneos*, 2009, by Iñigo Aragón

Interior Photos by Lisa Samuels

Variant excerpts from this work have appeared in *Datableed* (UK), *Golden Handcuffs Review* (US), *Percutio* (NZ/France), and *women : poetry : migration* (US/Japan). My thanks to the editors.

Thanks to Erín Moure for proofing French and Spanish copy. Any lingering errata I embrace.

contents

Feel as if you were defeated forever. Pay close attention to this technique, I beg you, for it seems to me that in trying it you should melt entirely to water.

Anonymous

The Cloud of Unknowing

c. 1375

morning

{1}

The warm breadth of a thumb pad lifted across her cheek in the lower night after her voice said to wake up from a disproportionate story of apartments, packing food in suitcases, billets of paper from a man with his acquisition service and a woman of indeterminate girth who kept appearing as she stuffed her suitcase heavier and heavier, the low sound of a foghorn establishing a base note upon which slowly her blood steeped, and the birds began layering it, the bag full of bread and pies and meat, sweet things too, preparing for a body of water she would reach: in the water the dark blood of thinking pulsed *telling her how to walk a path without literacy or numeracy in evidence, how to step with ambit cracks and tiny pinnate leaves* as when lying amidst broken lights, the apartment complex shines by sounds entering the windows of your senses in a dark plink call like soldiers near in caravans *you had better stay down where you are* performing whatever Act protracts the water's swole meniscus—at the window edge you hear the shout the animal sent up flying in the air by a vehicle that barely pauses becoming the inside of your torso and you fly up, flecks of dark fluidity cast the lower sky with shades and your social concern cracks:

how could they make a mistake she learns not to ask, wrapt in waking, the
first question to which one knows the answer untrammeled by cavernas in-
fernales del periódico in the cosmic situation of this room *designed for empa-
thy's internal destruction, the hit animal* with momentarily nothing to move
but the wayside, whose dulcet flats subtend Transverse Mercator moves,
drawing fertile bodies to the scene of spiritual consummation without
knowing how to manage the tearing of the heartskin *like those monks singing
waiwai in the tuning-stone hall as you sit in cloth imagining their sexuality,* the
tremendous radio blares softly next to her as you seek to assert some part
of your own, your skin there, amidst the self-exchange many early feel as
gratification or above, alongside, shot from overhead, infinitely projected
from the waterside streaming at barges that were ransom for other ghosts—
it was the same water, don't tell me said the long tiny body of the child who
basked in the bassinette of fire *so she came out scorched and never would be
the offspring of the queen of heaven she imagined she was, burnt beyond what
would have been her self-recognition* though she could not see anyone (least
of all herself), that would be a yielding of the title she calefacit uento after
all, the experiments in immersion severally presented to her whether she
accepted them or not, thus "acceptance" wasn't on the cards, wasn't on the
table or suspended bed here

near the sound of outside birds; she made her identity label on the case,
scratching softly lying on the bed, though she could not put her waking
body on the words at all, which she realized but only like the Ancient Mar-
iner talks about the ship dropping "below" the kirk and hill when everyone
knows she is not dropping at all but rather receding, or you away from her,
the horizon of where she starts turning like the top of someone's moving

head, después de todos los varios experimentos en la inmersión encontra-
da jadeando, disappearing into the crowd one last time after calling her a
strange bird, rāwaho, and giving up on the module of delectation that had
been their version of relating, ai

{2}

that kind of vision was one she recognized at the literate core, being then at
that time with children beginning to understand they were not beholden,
were in fact tethered with the lightest of implements, they could be snipped
like the bear or dog right where it hurt and fall gently from the real where
she was sitting now upright with her suitcase full of meat, anticipating
someone to attend her on a journey, a junket tally readied for the hour—she
with her packages and situations *I could tell you, she was completely lost in the
known, without a solid reference point for how she had entered values living by
her,* desire and fear long ago made available to gauge the land (floating pow
with zappers they spoke, lauded by their own selves being all copulas with
multifarious Elements of Reinvention, the young faces smile at each other
*and bammo it happens again, the moko chisels into the hill split down the mid-
dle* to tuck the batting in, as authority writ so well every second

we dazzle our selfs for populaces singing with horns placed loud in the
palace of suffering, knowing the dead are amazed by their own deadness and
call out quietly with faces still alive in their minds, stunned by the ground
their feet walk on amidst ours) here in the airy rain of a life lived simultane-
ous with hers though in another disputatio *as if bairns on ludes have suffered
enough, with those smiles we held in our arms as we prayed to the blue skies and*

the clouds with ideas of Sunday School penetrating our minds, generating like the batteries of Oppenheimer truly loins de côté, where her voluntary sisters peer their exigency and Love—

the room is clean, the windows very quiet, the lapis lazuli of generations braced around real arms and coiling up the throats of those she is both thinking to and being talked with, both sound and message in a synchrony one might recognize as an instrument's obeisance Elohenu, realizing the books written by the dead are only free when read by death, that your eyes moving wetly in your head are proper, banded in their real existence, and it's the ink of the imagined that creeps up your arms with its damp to say more than once a day you live and are in your bed, you live and are propped up by pillows of ideas, and someone near you says

actually metaphysics and physicality are doctrinal, like seeing words as literal and figurative as really the same, privados de su maleta de pie en pie para cruzar las latitudes de la autorización por las fiebres providenciales unknowing clearly sobre el océano o no esperar a generar (yes, y esto es lo dado, las fevers para nosotros un señal en los ojos in the tense surface): you don't even have to think about it, you just yield and the reflective posture has your stomach egress toward your tongue, wanting to speak to its pulsing muscles, to the woman drinking the water moving warmly there who's only free according to doctrine, binding the observer's idea of her face to the image's refracted worship

so be brave and synchronous, she conjures herself, don't give in to the inviolable darkness heaving in which the Lover moved from symbol to iconicity or the animal who broke *the tearing flesh of the animal that spoke to you* in watery syllables, the birds nowhere near strong enough to lift out her obedience when she needed it most: threads pulled toward the sky then they broke, the limbs of her mind declending, dark bushes moving in industrial defeat, the girl with cloth and the embroidered coach, the Lover moving spiritual merchandise made to yield

her limbs stochastic, unfolding to the vertical bright air's sharp ascent wedged in that "not-so-good" economy of day, that holding of the vehicular smile given over and over as the hair was torn by the dated machine and you had your recurrent experience of mismatch between what you knew and what it behooved one to know right there, right in front of your face held up *I admit it, I admit, the white stones under my feet I can't pick up anything, their luster by the construction piles so ultra light and yet I can't see them,* the day as bright as candy, clouds painted on the very far away sky—you were right I hardly knew anything, but one can be only in the part of life one has right there, in the body's tomatoes and vegetables and fruits and running streams, those documents that erase moment by moment, better than the

paling cars, the dented faces who cannot see the ground that binds their
legs and keeps them unrelieved until (she has seen them) their bodies grow
deeper and collapse their eyes from seeing their fingers dig into their brains
not heaving, not knowing or enduring longer, not like that—the wide hills
of snow, the wide wires of trees, the yellow flowers, the broken fence teeth—
nor by these do I mean knowledge like protruding mental shelves affixed
on giant geologic forms: though these move they move slowly: so when you
look at the propelling waves of a water: when you are crossing and you feel
the lavish movement of the water-ground: you might compare (were you to
be thinking on that scale), you might compare

the movement of those currents with the ready stones and rocks and shelves
of rock in the geologic strata one has seen in pictures or even up close: you
might wet your fingers and insert them into the strata of the rocks—or try
to insert them, for the stone will resist, since your temporality compares
then to the moving stones, you cannot see each other move since you are
rapidissimo fast and they inexorably slow—then your fingers will be rough
at the ends and that will be one sign

she's earned that rough, she touches the face and feels the soft roughness
(turns to the stroke, the touch a hypothetical know-cleft for the holes
in the head, the mouth . . . not the same as the heavy shelves, not that
slippage from the way her live mind works . . . so that "knowledge" *as
we call it* belongs to the dead who have stopped, pre-confederate, like
the spiritual orders of land edges in Maropia Manitoba Wairarapa or an

unnamed ground with language nowhere in evidence when you near its
bio-archive) particles enter the skin, particles whose sinews are minute
as the educators *know for their sakes,* they come in diffracted connectives
in hybrid dirt or the effluvia of salivated expiration, or daily logs, or
photographs, or habitations still visible in the earthwork we are digging
through—knowing that is not "theirs" but rather a recuperated tendency
to belief, a ratcheting mobility connective; so the only things we might call
knowledge, she thinks, are the secret facts of the dead that leave no trace:
nervio, mejora, improvisado, primal, no mercantilizados, construcción,
continuidad, the continuity of such clefts los nervios, lector de respuesta,
cerrados y abiertos: that knowledge is safe, untouchable serene, what the
dirt and animals knew whom we cannot revive, the skins of the never-
seen dead a great secret as we move from somber greys and browns to
a raft of crawlers and rock-garden fishes, we make the skin throbbing,
iambic, rippling, we make it gorgeously laden with the thick green of
outer earth—which also has this knowledge that cannot be activated

otherwise the pressure of the rocks, the force of gravity in your brain, must
endure the visitations of that mystery (supposing even that kindred to
knowing, *which we do not,* since, setting aside our fingers which have begun
to scrabble with the seams of the rockbed, *looking for the Word in the rock-
bed,* without knowing the starlight is coming toward us even when we put
our faces up to the showers of the trees, still, knowing: still

{3}

the invisible starlight shines toward her window, tiny points of thrill inter-
pose across the dawn median, acyrologia sinking in our skins and ferreting
out molecular subdivisions through our tongues, donde se estancan las
marismas, los ríos y donde nadar a lo largo a través el oscuro manto del
césped para codearse con sus amigos de la watery vivas estrellas brillan,
eyestone blue archive radiance: they build those castles out of water and oils
and sweat that transact *what I sometimes, silly me, consider some particular
memory or idea* as though separable from starlight *I sit here in the theatre of
my abode, language harkens me from the sublimity of my common clothes and
sweat,* dans ces circonstances elle prend des allures solennelles that herein lies
the altruistic shadow fully lit but without knowing

we are held to that litness: it's like the man who captivates his argument
with footnotes, keeping it tethered to observed experiences that render it
unassailable *per se,* as in a condition of para-endorsed magnanimous admi-
ration, dear believer, who yet sears the viscosity of human wishes with the
internal honey of what-has-the-bee-set-down and is thus admissible, par-
ticiples of eristic troglodytic verisimilitude—though fencible, beholden—
admitting their beholden state; even holding the hands of those footnotes,
their ascending arches, the sweet effability of their comparate dimensions)
counter-balanced near knowing and the knowable:

there's a phone, perched and twittering, feigning preen with slighted head,
hiding the entrance to the cave again where were the orthodox rocks, the
hand reach, the skin of the fingers holding

a dimension of preparedness tweaks in the wings *outside her decision to answer or not,* the crises rise bird gutturals, encyclicals, the textual phone call to the spiritual paraplegics, a welcome to the explanations attached to this scenario, watching the tall glass container full of potentially thrashing beings, *having been placed there no doubt* the biomeme as much a visitor as she is, chased and stirring . . . the issue at that time of whether or not to contact the authorities, to hide her head and turn away *but then how will you have language*

for her, as in the no-one-is-coming-to-get-you mode do you indeed turn from striving to doing . . . in the inestimable flatness of landscape wherein the covers were around her head and she was hiding even from requests to the living . . . the tweak in the window outside doesn't know what kind of answer it's going to get . . . flashes of wings solidly emaciate . . . . in a past someone is offering fruit she doesn't want or explaining how to make a repast without error and she doesn't care . . . . the natural effluvium of letting go is the determinant even when you see thought talents in a world where it's possible to assert control, over a little stream from what you make all the way to the Visitor having set sail in her as if she were a slip or someone looking at the window, she's toward the window on one side of the reverie, pressing her face on the cold phone; but the writer has not supposed that this phenomenon had any connection with free will, having answered the question of the paradox of the godhead knowing (and this unknowing claimster nonetheless experiences what is known as "will," figuring the real as bodies) the language of the cloud's dream manifesting through terminal interrogations *until you shake yourself awake to take a measure of your limbs,* inside their robed covering where she summons real feeling, where *nothing can justify a theory except it explains observed facts, simple as that,* en el libro las fiebres son providenciales, la gente espera o no espera, UP OR DOWN, ON ONE SIDE OR ON THE OTHER, el fuego quema para usted sobre el océano de espera o no espera, she's determined by la chica de pie en frente del hospital sin ningún tipo de idea cada vez más a generar (y cómo destruye la piedad) the body as those signs,

the birds continuing their multiple terrains in the expanding surfaces of air as they join one another outside the actual window, or as one perceives their joining: she holds her hands up to the air whose surfaces create those birds, the emaciate reaches of sound striving for a little lean-to amidst the hovering bodies, each one a wet inhabitor of equations, reaching sideways to take the measure of an equilibrium though *No Sanity Is As No Stasis Does,* we know, no bells crack, instead a breath flute in the room transpierces its interior silence, a radio drum's dub dub thumbed softly as her heart; the diadems of sonic pulse will transfer as they tumble by way of that person's tympanum to the veins of a leaf, to the top of a medial atmosphere, she thinks *all that distance, all the way out to the letter and back in again*

and who can divide them there, *no sane man can dream that the ratio of the circumference to the diameter could be exactly ascertained by measurement,* a group of those striving to do so having rubbed their eyes in replicas of this tiny place, inside the radio, in a locus before she's sitting here intervening to render visible the pained motions of muscles ceding to habits, cessation being their blindsight in that lay of the land you are looking for, forgiving yourself for wanting to be sure (because you copy death's immortal substitutions), stripped of that abiding self-foreclosure model holding in your flesh, forgiving your account of the multiple bridge clause between you and the apparently-not-you where no border operates; your contiguity plan has immediacy as its default *you forgive yourself for not enumerating exactly where to go out,* some juncture cleaved even today when it is raining with pock marks against the air

I am listening, escucho, *your face pressed against the cobwebs in the filigree, hundreds sleeping to wake up and claim a mind realizing how little we transcribe, how some embodied foundation is where* we walk, even with the molecular exchange arriving constantly this kind of wet imbues those functions *standing in the doorway convincing someone to join your spiritual psychology:* it's in the mouth, the children calling "am stram gram" outside the casa *when the guardian let her in to look:* nous sommes dans une ville *picking around the visions in which the heads of everyone are large dark oranges, pressing the air with no faces . . .*

so we *could* live projective without fail she thinks after the phone, differentiating the radio dial's fingering in which the Subject extrudes what squeezed partiality can, what softened roundness she must, that doorway like others shuddering against the Being who requires you *or as the pseudo visioner put it "necessity, love, and art had their time,"* the rain in pockets of heretical air, pressing to descend: as though it is her last-first day come on, "do whatever she tells you," come down, *come along,*

{4}

the sky is not so far up there where I begin, el ejido, much higher
considerations where the air floats until it ceases to be air and becomes
instead anti-air, canceled against itself because the orange-heads cannot
breathe, they cannot imbue each other with longing, but their relations
are maybe sharper, or maybe cooler or faster, those particles no longer air
brought down in clement horizontal press whose atmospheres fill up the
clouds and become really pressing, wanting to tell us something intimate,
picking up air clusters as the rain drops break out and descend, the orange
heads beginning to swell and peel themselves with arms *like when the egg
morphs out of the sac and pushes into the vegetable darkness thus,* similarly
the rain leaves its constituent cloud with gravity to descend, hitting along
the way some wind or torrent, joining other drops and pulling apart, its
air companions touching it as it falls . . . . . like being absorbed into the
lachrymose embrace of arms one's pulled into the deviltry of laughing
inside, suppressing it for love as if remotely possible

she thinks, thrumming the text in her lap, replacing herself with known
objects, the concept of the room an echo of the changed compassion
of *what's private, given* this woman prescribing future memories or
transcendental fixes to the offering half-prepared *you sing a resurrection piece
inside the period of this visit, having gussied up to show your acquired generosity
against the leisure habits of the worrying crowd,* the consummate enlightened
actants splayed against the inner wall of her head differentiating between
what she can manage to attend or understand; we must hitch up their
tongues to the side barriers of their mouths so they are not egregious, not
worried about anything because they have been sentenced, they know their

places as progenitive within a wait, the hasty hello kitty a substitute for the hasty goodbye, her long skirt moving around like an oracle, like who-it-is-meant-to-be as against the claim to perspective with which somebody thinks they landed,

it's nearly dawn rising and the transcript of my passions is all spent, here on earth I am trembling, the earthquake, the hurricane, hundreds of miles away at the dawn square, trembling it is—*do you believe me, kitty*—thin as hours go, speaking through the transom of my head as buried in mind I dovetail two fault lines backward at the curtain, my hand parting the congenital day, hungry for water I went then outside into the stone garden with its waters brushing against my curled feet and the sound of it wraps around my ears, my head directly birdsong with an accent I follow acutely a darling tendril of the flower right next to me for company, a key in the grass I'd forgotten from the visit; I traced and retraced steps, willing objects to emerge from hiding, those lost minstrels wearing mouthpieces with the first lofted sounds of morning water dampening my feet and throat, there I go up the gloated symmetry of the trees, against the pearled sky clement damp sounds of day on the skin in relation to its layers, beginning to converse, from depth to surface limbs, sitting on one's haunches stopping the blood from an easy flow to courage inward, and the synchronized electric warmth of the mammal which astounds the body where it comes from, the breath cloistering inside temperate mortality and hovering there *preferably moving as I said,* moving with thoughts of the wet dark, the hovering limit replicated by the trees nearby erasing the air behind them constantly and speaking *as I said* with the wind a middle-level whoosh scale, as though percussion's pale harp unties from its location

here in the wind it's dazzling, like in the pictures when you enter the screen and it holds your tongue and ears and torso and limbs in recurrent simultaneous, like as in or if you are sitting there giving yourself more readily than you do to almost any conversation no matter how beloved the interlocutor, you cannot remain focused for so long on someone's face or the scenery around it nor on your own readiness to answer (filter's ambient surface, the next question's so much more exhausting), even holding someone's hand at the movie house you are thinking you're expected to respond with the right pressure *you are thinking Ave, pseudo-Buñuel,* the stones building up weight from the chemicals that subtend that person's response, like you aren't really watching together: *ave,* that's the way it is walking in the golden wind outside here; *vale,* walk with me, the pavement where people are divided makes sense, and next to us the zippy transport edges stoneside where your legs extend the zone of the purchased citizen, the shared-taxation system that provides (her wet hair cloth, shake shake, the damp cleanse) the wet air carrying signals for your handheld satellite earpiece reverie while the wind lashes the signals constantly, *I think maybe the wind is trying to shake them out of molecular air* so she said then nous sommes allés jusqu'à aujourd'hui, cette ville avec son histoire de saturer le fascisme détecté les produits synthétiques breathing et les respirations dour, *we've gone far today* the peak of earth around that bend the wind scoops up your mana, mei Māramatanga, you're on the tops of the indentured earth walking along with strawberries in your lobes, under your tongue little strawberries, strawberries pushed into your skin the scent of your flesh moving upward to embellish birds in trees, dogs trapped in houses, leaves trapped on branches, limbs latched to the body, concrete sutured in-ground, houses skirted by dirt, bones settling down missing William Blake (fondling the stone in her hands) walking along impossible not to live, the clouds in front of William Blake partaking of multiple occasions in situ, adding to the known by tiny passage trials all that is made bullish and intermediate by turns the same vision from different angles: one an idea of futurity the other a knowledge of the tunnel into which we screen, the transformational movie on all sides as we walk the tunnel interwoven, turning our heads, radical logic in the dire eyes seeing copula visuals and defaced sounds and the cloud line jumping *zzzrrrr* listen to it, the sensation of the walking movie in which you never sit down, oh no, except when you're performing an action running over the embossment through whose guidelines she's extracting variables to hand to William Blake *as you move along, caressing the sides of the tunnel that bends the movie darkness* (spiritual readiness trembling in the approved text) *where you're learning it how to bend and what to show by way of closure laws, your dive-walk cupola sticks out of the film and out springs someone's job, someone's particular education, maybe a promised Lover,* the hair fallen out of the head or it's a wire from an instrument, a singing wire twinged so exactly like an artifice that tunes your death already there as passage

when the animal streams thought toward a visiting insect, she thinks, and you decide about wanting to squash it with your foot for disobeying the laws of your desire, to offer it an experience so as to increase its burden of responsibility for life, you smack a mosquito or an ant and roll it between your fingers because it's on your glass without permission; *but maybe you didn't mean that,* the live reel crawls out tinily and lands on your body with many secret thrusts and you press it, being kind to the thin density of the contact, her hand visible through the window light, the body looking out its frames; no you have no stomach for that no consciousness that the terrains of your flesh are inhabited by something you'd call other if it were looking at you by way of blood semantics, the chief tactics of a parodic cultural universe nursing a hope for the germination of seeds that root themselves in some anterior form that is not you nor no-one else exactly but that saturates what you're looking for, as you imagine-vivify the words given parlance by aveugle niveau parsed division streams *that lick the cool delicate eyes, stroking the ass, the breasts held up to water fully pummeling, stomach pulled back quietly the neck held and mouth wooed again,* those visions translate into letter's petted mammal gentle rocks observer pounded by surf taut bow held in the arms led firmly down quietened, maybe these words squeezed against the miniature canvas would unveil *figuras con paisajes* instead of those relentless evocative sirens, urgent bodily death and internal apologia (no matter how soft doctrine wafts your shape), a replacement of the sacrifices you made in order to be positioned like say "properly" have altogether released and freed her, for she lacks nothing, since she wishes for nothing, and nothing cannot be forgiven,

the evidence is everywhere in the room (hélas for Heraclitus touched repeated Lots, so sweet with stomachs to digest with flowering fruits to wash you down) without having given up anything a person would find acceptable, no no, these wafting-close-to-somethings are real delicacies of perception songs: speaking-reading, coaxing the alto structures *eating not fucking, fucking not making love, looking not* listing your body rushes back when you hear internal landscapes replacing disappearance in your ceding mind that turns to an orographic cascade for the dead lingering in your dreams by the wall: the unpeeled skin of the person talking to you then, all the blood and water that was within a desire to lunge or excoriate, to make that cultural belief engine light up, perceive a self-blessed meritocracy so imbued there's no hope without *explosion*

so the whole Mask of Life heals continually as you fall every day from a tree and scrape your back and you do it again and the skin heals ever so slightly by the end of the day you're at it again, scraping your skin and giving it back, healed and mollified by the process of demi-love, by the sacs of ardor in the skin that heals slightly every day *the words produce relation, your word-skin exceeds relation, the skin of the Book transpiring,* after which you pick yourself out of the line-up of your potential selves, ask for some music, maybe a soundtrack gloss or a consummation like narrative track thunder, a yelling peerage acumen delay, ideas about what is central *that sort of thing,* a youngster pulling your hand with an act that seems available, with a cookie or vegetable, with a mnemonic of worldliness like the sunny window frame from which she looks: even the sounds of nearby sisters heaving the fences, and how the sky above its corpuscles of clouds with its orange-head angels cascading time *the stooped curve back* over the stove laundry machine table bed digging variously through images on the dusty floor *costing more than usual,* the road outside itself grown over by hairy greenery, sister images opening out to the non-placating minstrel horas

taking many guises (spliced day sound images starting the boxed-out roars of suburbia opening garages, fully fleshed scenes feeling more okay than life right now, completely tent-staked with culture, feeding a thing you list one two three, your virtuous mind gone empty with how you're standing, what you've hooked your apparatus into for the warming food apartment in a line gone back pre-future but) then you say no stop no no, there there, now now

{5}

there is no future thinking none at all, the hardscrabble surface of the earth takes all our energy being here such pleasant dominion, scarabs in the hard-packed Book of Egypt told her porque entiendes las cláusulas de sustitución de la muerte, the hidden books etched inside the lungs—rocks on the smooth peninsula told her with their mind spun cool and sweet, socked away with the corruption of the Total Real spinning through pro-genitive bombs, the water rushing through peace abrupt and irreversible: it's a wonder things hold in this new dimensioned set called nation-states, this tinkering with bodies through the cultural dream—*I mean you wouldn't believe how often lately I have visions* and then within a day or two are . . . people with some kind of act foretold . . . but it's common, isn't it sisters: prosthetic selves unhinge (the letter's rapt hostility soft like the gunner's opened torso continues to connect the arm that wields the gun, eyeshot and hand holding: like when you connect however loving in a blood pact with the person your communicant: you cut your arm and cut that person *not hurting either one of you* and hold them in the suture, warm drops for innumerable plenty), the idea of the person you were talking to totally *unmans* any how-de-do bridge of a hundred words or fewer that takes you to them and they to you in paradigm, like your hair is the helicopter that seeks out the ground when you are done, your shoulders turning halfway toward life, through an infinite degree of her alternative and disallowed mass

the day replays the builders on ladders, seeping trees tickling low-hanging clouds, children's feet getting hot in the sun, the swishing strength of the runner in the trapped water flicking the insect's wing as it scrambles off the windowsill, the last breath of the perishing primate and the first of the new born; these excrescences we savor with our stories of violence *with even what I have written to you,* not authenticity but a fully inhabited pose needing a real death to achieve it, the bath scene the whisper hidden area at the edge of the room—*but what are the means to express, how much has to be there making the strange familiar, your tongue complicit with the writ* dispute, so toned and ruling the very last bastion, yes the penultimate night having held open the suitcase to receive the meats, me mordí el brazo y exclamé, after all as the strange investigates itself her arms hold that event, supplanted in a witness, clear shaft dormant in the googled laugh, clear strength door what-we-nearly parishioned, sisters, what you spleen on a wait protected from a violation from outside, where the ordinary feels most real *your flesh is all the thoughts you believe* you are a kit to add on, volition or desire double the instants you'll perceive, you'll see, you're going *in* to the time

{6}
before all this, before this she was walking next to the median with its lovely machinery of body, verde como una esmeralda, where she is sitting now breathing the syncopation of the letter *its intended reader also holding the achieved symbiosis of alterity, I mean the actual as projection, blinking eyes of a nomadic "you" that came out early in the mind,* she is reeling with it, sinks over to the dizzy atrophy of that reel

the screen sinks over the basin, the eyes roll to it, her blood moves ampish-ly fast as it needs to where the sink is still far away, her mind bobs up and down fetching all the warm sloshing near itself and holding the door's look, whose rectangle will support her paroxysms of seeing, eyes upturned toward an idea of who will enter when, the door like an enormous eyelid tilted on its side, the doorknob's point . . .

and beyond that the hills roll safety through, penetrating an educated guess about the woman walking, her skirts alive in air, that story of the ceremony you adapt so nothing will flange you right then, if you turn away it isn't real no one has seen you anyway the worker at the gate is permitted to say nothing that will change what happens (no one else sees the cello sheet, one thin pulse d'opacité, slip its arguments through the casement), someone you heard inside the washing cellular freshness mouths (again the tāina, a wet exchange of lobes talking) informationally, stringing less close to the foyer's humanity on display, everyone apparently recognizing exactly what's going on and still they stand admiring, smiling with skin turned inside out for feeling more acutely the hot inquisition, the jagged fog of temporal huff like a bird on glue on your flesh light feathers, the kind people breathing people—her flesh feels like midnight air unperturbed as the changed urban setting soars out now significantly later, the boys call from their shoeboxes they called to her not-answering self-issue, dominion scored in the paper (inside her revelation *people strutting make that move, their eyes instigating*) softly, they speak their perspectival sheath unreeled

that mortal smiled kindly at his glass, kind goggles transconnect to "serve" in the mode of replenished futurity (one could wonder what a culture does post-suture, devouring machines with a little perspective, membranes pulsing the very looping mechanisms that transpose your life stuff into bravery and power: maybe it's kinder to do the tree-stand bit, replacing context for breakfast, locale for lunch, world-place for the afternoon and animality for sleeping, all summoned by authoritarian fundaments offset by—persons gluing placards to their faces with gentle connectives as if construct could lead us) to some place you used to live *before you know it scattered* in response to that woman you saw standing in the dark from the import's tinted windows, the skinned man watching from a distance like it's a movie and a television show prolonging their time together, Electrons in Love, the dim fantastic like ping pong balls over your eyes half-lidded in the low story: you hitch up your sleeves completely interrupted when someone wonders why a border breach suddenly turns into a *logical outcome* giving persons or land a name

lugged up as blood: *look we believe, help us,* the stories of inclusion this blood can tell drinking Golgotha's immoderate stasis: living like that, sisters, we've amped before, immoderate gambit one neither "has" nor "gets" but soughing *dans un lieu élu* substantiate liquid folding out, holding the writ cloth the radio plays *through her future tears, behold the manuhiri cometh in history upon us occupied*

{7}

and therefore souls esteem no other state of being; thinking in her water she is saline sans Tiresias, weary with anticipation with having to explain, tiered with the birds *not exactly cooing* in the outside-a-window-morning though she thinks about those sounds, having sent that maybe final missive she is holding the map dripping on the suitcase, kū kū, coo coo, she's opened her heart to the interlocutor, the anticipated visitor *we know what that's been like, we say we are repetitive as we eat the globe in our hands like shape form quality weight location globular globular,* the tense shoulders sequester each other over wires that depend from the building's windows, her eyes drip through the wires toward absolution's condensary—the space around the people on the streets looking at each other over paper, looking on the street as when it rains (very near the chair she's sitting slumming now)—and her breath begins to open in the air that's gotten thicker and distending, her brain widens and pushes out its substances, her thoughts become pliable nomenclatures into which seep little chips of cloud that speak toward the trees whose leaves can't help sipping in and dropping out spots and patches of rain, bend and sashay, their branches getting very heavy like her limbs, then springing up, so rain's a rain of living *like your skin's a series of little drums opening slightly and shifting to let the noises in and out again, the brain opening* like a series of skies into which are explanations gently punishing a Tropic of Separateness, the fluxed omitted atmosphere; near the window her eyes are full of clouds, undue arrivals of the unplanned for, se puede imaginar una tal oscuridad o nube llevada ante sus ojos en el día más brillante de verano

for whom she pins her treatises around the windows to shine some light inside the ink, and the future rain paws them with softened diminution and plans are stirred and planted through the air—shiva labor, shivering though it's warm in here, she tempers her artefactual clothes, turns around on herself several times consuming soft idea noises, someone through the screen beating on the tail pipe of a wagon *oh manna oh manna* the cries come out dim at first and then increase in frequency, opulently pulsing, the brightening air interrogative about the burden formally on her shoulders,

a crisis magnetized by the messages intruding on her efforts to nurture Redemption's quires, to support tandem circumstances as if they Believe (*I mean "getting it right" takes all her energy now*) the clock ticking, the promising threat of turning upside down on the suitcase and having the earth this time above her wedged in the cloud, the cooing birds building air dams over a machine playing the sounds of history through running water, awa pahure *beautiful you hear, the waters surge through your dressings they are ready now, they've grown form and wings, magnified by a seriousness we bring to constancy, surrender oh my birdstar,* mate nama pulsing pulsing ohchganghooo very softly summoned, they spell it with a trill here, hemos fluido fuera de nos mismos committed to the ecology of self as devouring producing replicating, wooing the circle de la mitad que queda en su interior as a series of infinite recognition peeks over and over again, *so when you are flying over those pools listening to the birds oghrahncroo* a little closer, the roar of airplanes answering *when you are flying those birds heaving down on the branches with stone arias, they ventriloquize the stun of another person who imagines a Life of Not-Sorrows hold her safe,* dit-elle, animals without ancestors socializing a soft air, a seamstress picking her story, our lady of errata

swallowed the letter whose ink-blood distenses fluttering in her chest within her stomach, *that dull mass inside you* a blue-struck air meal woven in the pūriri, in the branches, in the gradual piling of those stones while she was sleeping *that I know yes you told me,* re-naming to put the phone in your hand, to own the information you were touching; held to your cheek it became an archive; held to your heart the camera could take a picture of your blood and transmit your situation, could step in here and show the floor and rocks and wooden walls volte-face inside ideas of defacement, resisting to hear intimacy foresworn—ideas visit her apartment, trying

to speak through the paper, the vibration of the paper with wet lips
thrumming near Higher Experience where the rāwaho and the bluethroat
shuffle in the rafters, shift inside the underwing of the building once
again, angling dependent wings against the wall outside her window

outside notis she hears them, the words grow blank as action's exegesis
drinks them out, the sentencers make her wait her summons, walk with the
same degree of consequence hocking toward the suitcase glowing with the
plump flesh of her skin's crochet, wet with the room's dulcet humidity while
doctrine salts array beneath her tears *no matter how long you fall asleep on
the floor with other people passing by waiting for truth, acting about where we
might or might not go now, released from a prior definition we depended on*

the Offspring itself, reportedly, looked around as though its mind were
made of windows *like those slim ones that occlude the outside view though
you yourself can see,* letting in daylight and permission, its whole face like
Foresight in which her internal destiny figures its obverse, the delicate
Otherwise—*no one can see you,* that's what the compound child thought
in its bartered moment of what it means to grow; she tried tending like
a sheep which requires the categorical ruthlessness of other sheep, she
tried retraining herself to abdicate, self-forgiven for the instinct of that
day: the set morning is a good place to do that, hemos escuchado a los
pájaros broken through the willingness of the flowers blown below—*you
can torch them if you like, if you want to, get away with it, think you can get
away*—waiting for the pattern of behavior in the natural world to return

{8}

its figurations line her radio, the tiny excrescenses every bit as expectant
as the spit sitting softly in the lower troughs of the mouth waiting to be
taken in *as you stroke your hand gently across your cheek with your thumb the
trailing indicator of where belief has been,* lithe and iconic (the sonic image
of the man handing her the papers to take to another country reminiscent
of a cultural definition of birds, smiling automatic the doctrinal follower
inveigling a hand inside the chest and making promises not to die, how she
replaced those papers with a floating translucent overlay blue revealed) beg-
ging anytime soon estoy un poco apurada, the fire burning the trees away so
assertion could be healed, la fuerte compresión de las escenas iniciales y el
solemne viaje del consul gives her disparity enough to keep distracted,

the morning keeps her company while she waits, construable Love hovering
upon her arm or mouth, *the eyes eating you out* deciding whether sacred
listening is most wantable, furniture marks gathering on the skin until they
are so accumulate *you no longer see consciously isla nuestra* con la avena el
orgullo en obscura planchado, vivas bajo el hilván, the sylvan hills tucked
freshly human-planned los labios me dicen la primera visión del entorno,
this soi-disant country sure of its pain trees clatter where they hovered ropes
for battle animals

(thus pain reserves itself for the new dialectic whose reflections keep her
company as she applies herself eagerly to this work of contemplation, the
spiritual animal showing with distended stomachs, with a kind knife held
to the flame to get totally clean *the way only mortal things can be perfect* in

her condition—even though she did not know, for she could not see anyone *least of all herself* arbiting form in the hermandad de la imagen; waiting beautifully soledad, she had been trained to recognize immersions severally present to the muscles of this woman pulsing with her fully oxygenated face

{9}
"free" as it is for her, conscious of binding the image that moves refracted inside worship's tethers *be brave when your material ideas imbued her statue, stella hau, your Common Envelope moving brackets nearer and nearer to the res public, breaking limbs and licking the flesh): *we cannot revive the animals, their bodies secret tangible not to be known* whereby the reflection in the window moves across the somber greys and browns to a comparison, coarse hair braided in to hers, gentle spiders and necklaces laid against a throbbing skin's iambic ripple, laden with a gorgeous lapidary, hidden by your legs near a stream of liquid confetti *where's a window through which you make out someone watching in a reverie* unconnected with free will or doxical substancehood, having garnered the phenomena in a cloth bag commonly associated with the godhead, spiritual traps being what they are for unknow-ing experience

dreaming through questions she leavened constituent clouds, as though gravity takes its chances descending, bumping the wind torrent joining invisible forms it pulls apart like air companions as it moves; she does this thirst in an embrace close to persuasion, smiling on the inside of the room tending the circuitry that another self was holding at the moment they dropped by the spirit house with a newish plan—ella no es la patrona, pero ella es la persona más amada—to be Somebody's baby, and that person, that intermediary saying maybe "this is the right culture, the tight culture, the psychogeographic mapped-out night culture" *that kind of remote hog-washed juridical wrath* that collapses when it gets overlaid in an environment where the light makes it very hard to see what happened, watching the moves come together and afterward wandering in the cultural wind, in the frizzed-out dynamism of internally divided people:

it makes sense, for being born in that house, it's a kind of invented wheel that vivisects the words: right when everyone shows the world prolapsed, how befitting our Experience, the yearning my sisters to "do whatever she tells you" in the posture new to experiment

the beings seek continually that solder burn and heal, they seek continually the aniam, a prestidigitation wanting to *know* the *non-scapular thank you* dress held to the water pulling it apart, the stoking of the genetic fire dragged up toward the Garden where the water feature symbolizes itself, the stomach held tautly to make your muscles pull the scene apart, as though ex nihilo arms and throat visions repatriate with words on fire the screen *that* doubles as the token for strong argument:

dark as it is, slate against her picture, her suitcase sideways to her lower legs, held around the table set inside her mind spelled back into breakfast, the day having reversed and the food re-instanced in her mouth, wet bread torn through milks of consequence one would not notice any such thing; you list the virtues of belief on the sides of the slip in which you'll cross the water, listing those on a paper boat her throat has become, a sui generis matua brought some time ago, the rose windows torn now an image of their tact held together, words scribbled in the forms of photographs . . . she "empties her mind" into an image of *hermandad,* a gathered image held together by the near similarity of the substances around it . . . *your mind a single image, conveying or defending against or seeking "the present"* . . . sitting on the edge of the bed, veneration lathering itself on patterned sheets the community gave her a time when her illness was too productive, these histrionics rule her internal eye so that she momentarily cannot see in front—or that eye will meet the visitor, the doorframe showing visions of the believing yes

{10}

one might call her theoretical interlocutor an experience en la casa de las acciones voluntarias, en el medio del océano de la cama: *investigating violence as meaningful form, the being in front of you tries to say something; but you cannot speak its language, so you separate from yourself in order to increase* el crecimiento de la población limitado a la probabilidad estocástica meant to be performed or witnessed in silvery shirts and feathery midriffs and ochre-baked interiors, with little fish for breakfast, soft bread for lunch, warm meat for suppertime and solitude for sleeping, a content regimen sometimes upset by the appearance of variety, large placards showing forth allegiance, *time to freshen the doxy* as if experience defines how you connect (*if you follow that sort of thing, depends on how your animals trill or scrawl or fillip, whether the skin of your inner eye is on the lam*), she looked a little closer when the quadrilateral dosage stroked that hand, the caravan door dangled open and people fondly attached to death revealed, however holy, pleasant, or consoling those thoughts might be

as for the first time a soft air stirring at the house, birds clicking against the terra cotta, a wooden spoon against the side of the bowl in which she stirs the food she'll eat, eggs and milk to join the butter, the stomach in a relation to air until you wield the food with it and suffer again the distinction between caveat and strength, a branch of conversation in the Names for Things, one in cultural grooming, some touching definitions, enough recognition to accompany the centrifugal music this time of day, knowing the pleasure of asseverate company the spoon hovering mouth open in response to a question it answers; she smiles blanks in a cosmic tramp through the situation of breakfast—

having taken an educated walk in that future day, finding a form she put to her head to see the vortices of inner sight empathic and institutional at once *like a hit and ride,* the bluethroat sweeping down so its wings can eat particles in the air, pinnate dunes situated by craft, the roadside baked by covering stories in Katikati or Caterina or Catskills or la tierra prometida, a moveable set of eateries with little mouths beneath them mercantile in the sense of an exchange for developed leisure at the natural, young bodies moving one direction and another among everything increasingly the length-to-width ratio leads to differential calibrations of time, i.e. spiritual years are exponential *she was explaining to the listeners without having to turn one side or another,* the blessed food in her mouth, her bag in the room

sinking like the Venetian sailor preparing for departure with a folded situation, like a letter written or received *as one might say, the map unfolded into the known world architects could tell you* stella hau could be her name, of the long eyes applying exaggerated cloth to dark lines made from muscles having no acid left (the sacred limb whose glassed recess heaves back the air), moving her terrific image constantly refracted even while worship's bright and wavy to disperse the fluttering trickster, who arrives and departs in a simultaneous spiritual act, the room where you pronounce "imbue" and "sacrilegious" as they're taught, estoy considerando lo que pasa en mi cabeza tan apretada a veces; her Active life begins after that moment como hicieron hay anos a mí, algo que era tan dolorosa para mí, somos amigos contentos más que de cruz, aún más que el callejón donde *your smiles convinced me, hefting one book and another in the bluestone cloth* you float the books through air while your body goes down, down, down, down, down, down, down to the bracket of the floor-cum-street

{11}
with threaded fruit all over it, the sweet flesh of the blossoms getting stuck in the text and still the tournament of pleasure to attend, you and your sisters, you and your plans took the road whose switchbacks fleck

the caravan with the temporality of stones, you breathed guardedly in this moving slip relation

the edges of the cliff can't see the rock inexorably moving, "wait up," and the caravan going in situ in between you when the driver smiles nervous holding fingers graceful to the wheel, rough at the ends from tying spiritual knots *grown to a life in signs,* you adjust your headgear in the constructed room scored with a land tongue *Aroha mai, aroha atu*—

it's strange you know, knowing, which we do in the starlight, knowing in the sunlight with the single plane curving once, all day otherwise alone overhead while you hide your nakedness in the seams of the rock nearby the cloud which knows nothing, either the stones or the hidden cliff dropping down, a layer of dirt falling over everything like gauze, gathering up the lower legs and traversing the bottom reaches of the scrabbly trees that interpose between the very thin wires that connect the very thin paths of water that are trading places as you plan your route, tiny points of thrill coming across the medians, a vision of the known touches

rising up from the papers in front of her face, the gentle blood going down the thighs whose waters answer to the buried river free of ruse, a stream from what you're made of (on the opposite side of the reverie the sister went to the market to buy bread, cheese, oranges, the dusty woman, her hands turning into wings of paper the constant sin for which she's suffering innocent) pulled apart, *which I can understand that* "yes but where do you make the lines" wavy, the clasp in the middle of the blue event when everyone disappears but her idea

and an opposite unknowing manifester of no less experience convincing someone, a Psychologist of Hell content to hover in the doorway during sessions, a bowl of fruit on the desk whose emanations press the air with recognizable smells as though people were turned into Topics, d'un moment à l'autre des regards le votre sidéral, story lines that were failsafe pressed upon the rivulets leaving marks in that doorway

near which someone thinks they landed cut through sheets or cells of magnificat, the buildings trembling nearby as the earthquake hits right at the moment your interlocutor had a Revelation, emanations in centripetal sublime—*do you believe*—inside the transom of her head, dovetailed in the mind like a knife held in someone's hand before,

{12}
you try to watch the future rain falling from the curtained ceiling in a daze, her legs walked sanely then through currently nonexistent fairways, pretty full of pavement people as dividing marker strategies where the road, where the cart, wheels out from life formations parallel to the stick

you spring into position, ghost life mashed into the soil of the walls not unos "pueblos" más bien una cara con los ojos manchados, rino kōwakawaka que el fuego que quema hacia el exterior, sin motivo, elation suppressed for the sober tread as she sat there filling in a Response she was supposed to—had she received it in time, before dying in that future—read in the position where life was gloriously spread out before her doing the work of Contemplation, microglass and cloudstone everywhere around

while on the radio, the box incoming, someone was talking about the medicine we take when we think we are going to get to a Somewhere that will reach the circumambient part again but it don't, *it doesn't,* un lugar tan perfecto comme la miasme sensory charnal apparatus devoted to increase

the mistake you bothered your brain withal, the blue wheel life sport muttering under the breath "I am innocent of the circumstances of my life," the conviction as though an apparition rose for her blinkers and then vanished, a constant tourist Lover shrine there already streaming tweet tweet, piwakawaka *when you spread your hand not knowing if it's a bird or star or flag* moving overhead or even toward you (disobeying the laws of smack or hunger, your encounter laced with rolling the vertical torso toward the next alcove

as though the woman with energy roils between the body and when it can or did speak, the world finally truly upside down and all the water falling into space, the internal landscape dark and salty like the stars out there meeting with the crust of your body's crystalline displacement or pseudomorphic matchings within and without, en el presente puede contemplar una restitución, disinventing place she is not disappeared, yet she is not anxious in disappearance; real as the same dependence this is her being "relaxed" as she walks the in-ground flexible maze of the sacred mistake; a giant shape speaks kindly carved inside her veins without will, ratcheting without discomfort as she's chiseled in to the memorial wooden panels heart thunk, heart thunk, heart thunk

in a bought-at-great-price mind hovering with the virtuous local Hurt in the Now, this woman smiles with presence built by a series of human waves, a physical world on which her body stakes the ground *breathing next to you* an importunate safety far removed from the regular lethal walls of the Fair City, her subject properties nullified as proposed

unowned, it's a strange thing, the man at the stairs by the sifting plants, the woman with the scars taking off her shorts, birds playing tribalism, one set of trails exchanged for another custom sharp fulfillment, the woman moving her legs over the long cloud having breathed out through the phone *you can't believe unknowing that's going to get you:* meanwhile noon animals hooding place, the prance books wearing jackets, showing their love with placards gluing labels as if connection, stella matutina, were enough in the

afternoon

when it was clear another court room could not be man-
aged, our mouths adrift in the violent angle of the living
room, right in the center, the corners of the room visible
to my eyes realizing my mouth would fit in again; you can
say no definite words though you have choices, you can
put the book near your heart within your shirt or you can
speak to the jacket that has grown a throat and arms and
walked out through the swinging door, out the air and
breathing in an origin not her own *down the dusty path
where the donkey died its familiar death, its legs open like a
willing sexual partner not quite knowing how to move, an
interior extruded for the theorist to consider* near the pale
rocks eat and be bountiful, thank the animal as you tear the
thigh, define the encrustation of bone, weigh your hand
against the lever of your elbow as you anchor your appetite

on the table promising not to move until her saturated scaffold
takes a dive, pulls those rural ignitions (mammal skins sucked
inside out, vegetal husks turned into dolls) making promises
not to disintegrate until parity with the known is recognized
even for, like, point six of a second, like the particle accelerator
tube the work is just volatile enough to keep her mind on
a path through doctrines of a Sorrowing Transient; certain
photographs certain hoverings over the mouth at the seam line
of her suitcase, the room beyond the room being where Real
Arguments might stick, the furniture achieving parity with its
also-present future evanishment, documents from the mobile
man servicing his cultural children determined dirt, measuring
their girth to keep appearances in heaven whose uncreated
spiritual being engenders nil jointure by compare

avec d'autres planches "I mean keep them, there is no one
else," to me loving means loving you said the person as they
stuffed their bags to leave, the heavy sound of the shared taxi
establishing the departure note that would play in one's head
forever after each time someone left, upon which other tones
began to sift, the meal getting cold on the table by the papers
massing polity, the bees outside layering their works, the shop-
ping bag empty and ready to be taken in again, pita and tahi-

na and oranges, sweet lemon cakes, the gathering of beings
angling matlines even if they don't use those terms since que
fueron incluso leer esa nomenclature's always partial where

someone was concerned, the women were praying aloud
in tongues with primary vocalics unlike the tremolo or
divergence one hears when persons replace themselves with
instrumental sounds, *pushing the air wet forward from their
mouths turned flay* the day cracked with brightness and
now a woman is sobbing without being able to stop, she
heard someone say *she must be under a lot of pressure* and
then she understood compassion, *anyone might have done
the same thing* even when her temperament summons Petra
habitations cave-like, ready to intervene, the danger blinks
with an expression sucking inward

as though events inhale themselves then spin out other sides,
accounting for the day she stood by the road trying to hail
a moving sign—but they see you, they know what you are
and *will not stop,* another vehicle barely pausing affirms the
occasional necessity of silence and you speak with your shut
firmly shut now mouth that firmly apprehends the rules
for the duration of the ride, flecks of moving fluid re-cast

her skin in a glow and the lower sky without ceasing to be
venerate also becomes social, *how a mistake is learning not
to ask or a water body hammering* at the same time *el agua y
las galletas están ricas en su boca* telling select persons whom
you imagine might have seen *the girl hazarded in the basket
that resembled a suitcase: she would never have the blanket
and the ring, she would have the chance to be pleasant for the
Number of Her Years and then turn* cognition's lathe, actives
to be forgiven, they can't help "doing" *ur texts for productive
dominions* sweeping through lithe battery tsunamis

under their own obligations to a thick present covered with
mud, the board nearby covered with smears, we can't forgive
cultural codes their violence whether they know it or not, I
suppose they become inscribed like present-day authenticity
requirements as though everyone's a journalist of the now, the
person at court to whom you uttered bluethroats fluttering
up out of your eyes, unable to rupture the wall you hold close
to your chest *it's like a room you carry everywhere* the person
squeezes shut at the Small Town Restaurant, like someone she
could not explain anything to *y el único ejemplar*, as though
she too thinks she can't be tongue-tied, the walls replace the
predictive absence of

integument—walking by the Organization being recognized
after calling on relative strangers to unsee, with the edge
of the land tipping perilously close to national license,
crumbling at the border that substitutes for *cultural belief*
structures called acting and admiring, that consolidation
of belief: you are the values done taking you up: eating
and being eaten, a Strange Bird with spiritual lactation
understanding mammals *it doesn't know that word's in fact
holding her*—actually tethered and forcibly aware like when
it hurts they turn gently from the flesh-wood in the way she
remembers, though a blind made of skin was laid over the
eyes of her heart

she is saying open, *open, go out* go out real plain spoken
the authority was all like "it was ordered that the door be
opened," and you with the seconds of hesitation and the
populace singing and re-imagining the stories of muses
*Christ you were even reading that shit at the same time, forced
intellectual capital poured into your domain, more word
machines and gizmos* generous with their torsos of gold, they
could reach with their own necks bent around the horns
we played in the palace of suffering, the soft fronds of the
wicked painters beholden to no-one now enough time has
passed, the Guardians of Earthly Malfeasance amazed by
their callous imaginaries toward the table spread with bones
the dead names call to us: indigo, amaranth and Tirangi, her

frill hair dazed by intellectual heat ("not *this* way," said the
letter to the pyrrhic Beloved) like art; long before this new
letter got composed, here in the room she sorrowed over the
question with no reason or judgment, the scarf held lightly
over her face, the cellophane carrying its message through
the casement

whose wood frames sundered flat against the wall held up
calling us with fresh faces still alive in our own minds . . . her
feet on the carpet preening by the ground near our own feet
lovely and bare . . . wearing the feathered text with cloaks
made out of spinning women not even seeing anymore
(their smiles held quiet while people thumped occasionally
by the door, ante los brotes abiertos de asombro en la
plenitud de los engaños ofrecidos dolorosamente touching
her with ink propped on pillowy ideas of freed memes)
kei te pai ahau, when actually it turns out physics is allied
with the phone's placated breathing, acutely *we were paying
as much attention as the next cultural implorer;* because one
senses words means they're always literal, literal, literal,
literal, literal, and really the same figuration teaches you to
see the mirror when arguably no one's there, you don't even
have to think about yielding your reflective composition
lai—we were listening when your tongue tasted Higher
Experience, *we have a match* for an event you intensely

behooved right there again, kaore he roro e rite ki to the impressed scar in the forehead grinning held up right to that admission, looking directly at the spiritual target punching the boards beside your shoulders with the force once used to make caged freedom, a will pushed to the decreed limit hit invisibly

she cannot implore anything else after that moment with the toxic statuesque, the bluestone luster by the curls so ultra white *we hardly move in looking at the picture,* the committee firm and vague in its assurances utterly blind to "the best part" dreamt, the statues rendering her fleshly dimensions artificial, her arms here and cold, rendering percept with no actuarial substance nor portion of regular being *in whose visit you feel your body is a Free Land whose inverted commas pinch the centuries,*

inside the Dome crushed with carpets is the cradle under the stone at heaven-tide; you stand for a principle of devout non-compliance though they're coming for you; you try to move and just like in the movies your outline begins to disappear the Land of Reality decreed for you by ideas buried

everywhere you walk, your absorptive torso cross-hatched
by the exoderm of thin gold struck right there in the body's
fruits and comparatives—you know, you feel, understand
more than you say:

you were to be thinking, scaling the soft side of the hill
comparing one set of waves with another, that shockwave
with this wave of wind peeling off the clouds, getting you
ready for the moment *she's in the photo pulling the blue cloth
up over her head, smiling like you're here,* ready movement
of the stone shelves across the backbone of beliefs in which
your strata sees in pictures right up close, mightily taken
with the detail of the fingers and their tearing velocity
compressed in fluid vêtements—she can't see any of this, the
cloth soft on her face, the high clock gently gonging, and
this not seeing makes her see perfectly; she knows better than
to resist so much arriving; the corner where she's standing
takes a while to yield its temperament *though you had your
head then in one of those fantastic-century vegetable bags with
the mesh through which it's difficult to see* nor breathe, in
which the diffracted connectives became your theology ever
since that Sunday were translate: "I have stolen the torso
of the desiring city, I have animated her ready limbs affray,
a spiritual camera anchors the deity's mirror who once

considered her ideas fair"; not knowing how to tie things her
hands deploy permitted words *imploded by words her anterior
conventions don't authorize you to say*

one way or another, the night will come on to her with
syllabic multiversals, names with embedded images at the
base of the earthworks still visible, *so you are here in the
shred room watching* linked to those others where the food
is—was—made, where the statues serenade the silence with
disburdened tears, not hateful but innocent encumbered
with no sound, while in this earlier time she went then

digging through a row in which there was once a sacrament,
a battle harvest, once a non-verbal animal *styrax volutes
having become active, connective on a ledge I suppose* tracing no
leave to act, touchable pressing against the rock that's been
warmed all afternoon by a sun whose talk links fire eyes to
flame mouth: oho, a hand-hold separate without arguments
on the side, keeping it together for observed experience *per se*

like a paraplegic thought whose intensity is exponential to its
impossibly dear wish, the internal honey is thrown by blue
light in the bowl near the window, her whole skin smiles,
the sun shards tense in the door knob crystal and very secret

words pressed all round her head, hidden from requests to the living to be weak, enjoy that weakness, mercy peace with inflex justice: the window is blank and gives answer Tainui

to explain the effulgent letting go outside someone's reaching in a pocket to get something really bad for you on a very attractive continuum, drip drip, the stratagems pulsing sideways by the pull of one person's heated ice to the veins of another with a drip drip drip the rain comes to the heated chair's sane man asserting the ratio of need for—*even today raining with air I am listening to your face pressed against my cheek, my sisters, the warm statues claiming my mind with diadems, the mirror reflecting us in that cool stone room with the simultaneous impress of the absent body,* realizing in her walk among the houses, mueve la cabeza al pensar en sentarse en la silla peluda junto a la pared verde del espectáculo drinking the liquid, immersing her insides in a willed conversion trying really hard

we were in a molecular transcription kind of wet but otherwise good to go more sharply or with more compunction pressed by atmosphere wanting to call out "tell us if you know something; what's that like," about air for example, how it clusters with rain and drops, breaks out, descending when your eyes

emerge like rays pushing toward the scrutable, and spying
it thus and similarly your head making all the difference be-
tween what exists after your balance trips over the equivocally
hitched tongue—a kind of bridge to the side barrier of the
head land *she can't be worried about the sentence coming from
outside progenitive's "whoa," what comes is* not at all hasty,

a greeting to the substitute teacher of a small particular day
whose long skirt moves sympathetically aloft as the morning
passes for afternoon, "whoa" the interior courtyard gathered
in its stones, the swish of fabric below the window between
the well and the woman sitting . . . far-off noises . . . cher-
ishing the aging children ranged in clusters *here comes water*
dampening your skin freshly, your throat drinking and your
skin scampering on the delicate foursquare machinery

fitted along a pearled sky so natural at the cellular level you
shift in the line of the suitcase, your tense eyes wrap around
the damp sounds of rock, concrete, steel girders, nice filling,
smooth walls, paint, furniture, screens, stone heft thick devic-
es holding each other, calling to each other in between (that's
how they hold, they call each other, our own dial-a-molecular
substitution clause, like we want to be turned within that
held insistence lathe, like the chapel is inside the residence,

the back chapel inside that casa sacred to her body) like the
dermis is the last opportunity of the mind to glow depth all
the way up to make a new surface of limbs aflow, un sueño
en que las cabezas de todas las personas eran grandes naranjas
oscuras, the room's like that al presionar el aire, sin rostro
one's haunted cathedral head having turned the greatest
possible harm into good

as she slowly turns her head, looks at the window flood by
day, an easy screen made out of fabric dazzling your cheek
and arms and lips recurrently giving access to converse, how
much the Beloved walks with *you flinging toward that walk*
the interlocutor . . . you can remain longing for the scen-
ery of that air, longing for that tideline with its exteriorized
trees where you hitch your cloth to the question's exhaustive
signals . . . her plebiscite (since she is wholly at rest, for ne-
cessity knows no law) winging its way toward Authority who
with paper ears wait ready

constantly I think, wind shaking through molecular rafters to
the other side of the wind, holding in the cloth with your lobes,
under your tongue little fabric leaves you keep there even in the

pool under the dry trees, the corner of the city tucked there by the walls, the cool obsolescence of the clubhouse that was awfully big then, you hear it has been torn down and you pad over and

peek through the fence put up so tourists cannot see (but you do), your physical self enmeshed in the burglary, straw shuffling your feet gusted by no food nor water, the luscious scent of cannon-balls

reaching your degraded nose reforming an episode of stability inside where the window can't see it, the sides of the tunnel new directions telling about how far to bend and what to show

the funnel that tangles us, camaradas, malgré cathartics' "I can walk away any time I want" from meaning, the paramount tactic of a guide prescribing tentative hope for the seeds in

your mind whose vast anterior sprouts make products of a shared identity: "our history" makes Casements, dark mirrors, hemokai for Tasks, people whose contingency tendrils push out

stranded to the core, you look on the window frame whose bubbles salivate toward those whose rungs have eyes across constricted wood, heads mashed together fingering ngare, kawara, part of a map written from underneath she's studied from inside

Proposals, Theme-based Papers, fragmento de epígrafe en griego,
that forehead shirr you rub repeatingly: what spiritual mirrors
do we'll not complain about in the building where we're
forcibly healed and growing backward tāniko gentled, that
worshipper rejoining the womb's visceral mouth speaking
without patrol—so she's meant to be sorry for the introjec-
tion of a body not her own, dear Earth

confessing to the stone cloth of entanglement, bearing the
letter made of flesh *with which she writ*

her body's conviction in the form of that letter

something we more than see, peeking in a room *close to*
you, waiting for the paint to come off the future walls and
preempt our design for nouvelle devouring, trope inheritors
constantly *showing you how it's done* on the other side of a
wall *who does not see,* not to be admired but portable, ordi-
nary, someone out the back of the house starting a car, your
head stuck as far in the corner as not exactly to make revela-
tion come into its own

like someone released from prohibition into selfishness, more
like (you could say) the loving animal particular, lowing
sweet with multiple convention digestives, walking on a path
narrower than their girth with wafting delicacies of percept,
haehae, cuticle, papakura, acarids close to ions jutting off
your body while the skin heals ever so slightly again, healed
by blue sacs of ardor (again, the blind replacement complex
passing-on, uncovering your face to exude communal past-
times from your flesh), after which you ramp up quanta's
substrate for

approved scenes that feel okay, mountains displacing hills,
roads displacing rivers, hills fences; this afternoon she
checked the literate scarabs to hear, the spiritual mouth drip-
ping its salvia down from the neck of the plant whose flowers
are actually pupae in the thousands, looking like the marma-
lade pins of peninsulas from the skin of space, *who told you*

"I got the parcel and I'm sitting here a moment before my
day becomes acceptable," she treads the note beside its
evidence una serie de objetos de adorno, personally we wear
*ever a nation of purr and stillfulness, all rhetoric and floss tinned
to hold you* connected with Some Kind of Love, whether a

blood pact or a set of persons who share a name or way of talking or cutting things *I mean who would not want to save our primal life,* our arms beautifully disgorged from wings

while you wait to respond to the request *he told her then many stories they gathered up in patterns like innocence* rejuvenation, stories like love without any people, the hill scene shining at the edge of your fusion—strange familiars on your inner body where you do not plan for anyone to look making you dizzy with the shared blood mending los death, still soothing at a moment's mind, a sheen rolling over the sound amps up—as a caul waking from a cold morning to the middle of a day far from where it thinks it should be, the sink hands holding it now heated in the sun, far away from where no one's watching, fast with glinting light the dermis knows nothing *per se,* scores up and down the tilth where you are pressed, magnet-like on the granite and held by duty to the surface pull, sloshing all within the warm body, the cool night yet to come,

the door closes that direction anyway, planetary skin acutely lured—by turning inside out the suitcase of the body looking for the parable edge as she lists (reflecting her presumption in the letter's skin), breathing, the escutcheon preserved by voices calling out *hey we can adore together* (in effect they call out "can I get me summa that" widely near the transport shed near the pseudo-house where the angles hold the walls)

you can *hear,* learning in your capacious bridal hoodie to call the names and rave, to stand beside people looking at the wooden screen shepherding any minute now vertical to each other, inhabiting only the zones of life where you're told you are allowed, standing still for the steel straw stuck into your head to suck inhale the free thought from your mind

thus the Indemner replaces himself with everything he's read, aphasia discourse pearling the clouds, humming the human throat sounds that push out over congregants eating Edenic compost, our shoulders softened by agreement labor one place at a time til we imagine "they were one-ing in the west, poring over manuscripts at large wooden tables, feeding our soul holes driving the animals while listening to literacy being opened by" new animadversions with leather-clad arms at the coiled sidewalk, looking behind us as we leave the gunny sacks pressing squeezing very slowly down, reading the letter—perhaps right now—tendering slight forgiveness for the bearer,

the rustling dresses cloistered in the door-framed gallery
looking as she adjusts her headscarf visibly reset *looking at the
hands squeeze out the sun,* greensward faces unremitting *you
keep moving around you are everywhere that's been, that's the
door* all that skin left behind to keep the place warm, friendly
cells on the floor your skin begins to recognize open wide
to reappearances, doing and failing the omissions of arriv-
al (since she's already there) pinned to the wall around the
windows, her hair like gouache curtains (where it used to be,
before the tight coif fervent pulled it back) some light inside
the wood instructions planted in spots through the spiritual
air shivering with pulses, her heavy water way within *turned
around* the documents of more proof

vacating: a whole life's staycation in vagrant pools that
contain each other outside underneath and overtop; *recogni-
tion* listening to the wooden figurines, listening to the shrill
invisible sounds of satellite radio chockablock piling on your
skin, conducting so much better now it's scored with crunch
vibrato apple blossom shavings, cinnamon shards, sand bars
rubbed well across; *grown up:* though he declares *become as
little children toujours les blagues de potaches* multiplies the
bodies of who's responsible

ka tatari tatou i roto i te heke mai still trying to conduct the
diving birds visit the window all afternoon in talking they
might or might not go now *someone is inking the building
with a sentence,* devising surfeit moves whose improved
didactics hold her still as stone;

the fluid on her skin's expectant, soft in the troughs the
mammal strokes her hand across the cheek whose thumb's
an icon venerate in reflection (a vision of Claude Cahun
looking up in the year of the dragon), looking out the
fringes of her soul with an inward-striving hampered planet
*into which you'd bite the morseled word seeking its creamy
syllable* notre désire clair pour l'entrée now since everybody
out of la machine infiniment drôle qui constitue le corps
—the sound of the siren advancing, bubbles in her stomach,
bubbles in her sharing drink cupped thenar held for glow,
containing

a woman
tearing in the vert room, taking to cultural deities like a
storm in robes, in fine bravura *darling* such wafers folded
in an envelope and mailed in other circumstances forted all

their own like aforementioned deities flowered into altérnate
form like petals fused through glass, like a ball or oblate
spheroid swooped with inkdust (thick-ish so they'll break
loud when they fell)

she is ready, therefore, to lie where people can feel, present
like, say, you know, you could be cement shaped to the diatribe
your windows made of cloth and awe, the haptic fit of spiritual
Love held by her devotion to altérnates por favor, the scent
she dovetailed with symbolic ceramic switching hands with
awe kāpara: will you *turn over your head and tilt the glass on it
when you are alone so you can* wear translucent's substitute,

turn your lungs into interior wet wings kū kū cooing and
rupturing each other like a deleted bird, the thinking
person's Tainui womaned in this pod toward seeming fruits,
strategically positioned near texts of innocence *finally having
uttered a whakataukī of close relation* you can smile laughing
non-sectarian, bending over into the laps of trees, your mind
bending around the trunks, bracing for an arterial skimming
blade that turned that life into furnishings, we can lie hard
on the winnow parser whilst

bending the laps of books her hair grows longer and
commingles supine on the bed where she is waiting, her
strands serving as ideational actants *the hair is a thought,
is* newly crittered particles of light on the interior scene,
you take your whying consciousness and there is touch
as os coercion or violence *such a mimic so squirming* that
long held super-question quite taut in its riveted sentience

mixed toward that assembly when she douses her body
with the metal pan water and blue cloth turning white
your eye-mind walks among it, yearlings by the windows
having held their tiring arms hour by hour wherein the
stones have broken through to voices again, her body being
washed with cloths the walls decorated with a black gold
forest established in our books, undoing certain relations
of a landscape,

lying down
with flickers in its eyes from looking up at the red uni-
verse which, literalized as given, those declaring angles
arrived singing "to give you content" recorded as organic,
stumbling, the city on the edge of its obsequies *pierced by
mental stars* becalmed on watery experience; in fact the

windows of her current heart were made like that—she's writ this in the letter—the mortar of heretical books mixed with the ashes of non-survivors and prinked out in mimetic reds and blues, and being of such stuff she encourages commitment when the daylight moon invades the window afternoon with signage some might follow *to the festival of the self-healed saints* (getting round that trial with doubtable frenzy, ascending nous allons nous sommes looped in the welcoming Festive Supplement) calmly supine again

drying in the air on the tight red carpet or half-held-up half-back, as though on an elbow of the spiritual galaxy *greatly reformed in dousing lavish intent* to remake belief as an autonomous art called out with silence: "I *mean* episema fluttering in my mouth, that's how I speak-sing in the air waves more tonally than when we were pupils in the Foreign City" where the buildings were impenetrably good looking in their height and breadth *and your genitives were part of the global extension of the second by which one makes oneself turn round with synchronism:*

these are categories of a whakapapa captured in the mystagogy water poured in tall straight glasses through which we then peered—ABOVE ALL DO NOT MISTAKE ME FOR SOMEONE ELSE—at the world turning into a Great Sky that stands above what it means, a second strand in repertoire like as if the ceiling were skeletal growth patches

broken toward a digitally spiritual infection some get through
indirection some perform grim-visaged,

unknowingly nearer to R&D her torso's sheer in the
philosophical extent (ah it's become the whole torso now, the
glass it balms and spreads, like liquid from the door) more in
keeping *if you look at the list where you'll see more* surprised,
enfeebled, deranged, or turning the cloth-text into uniforms
recruiting for hungry brains: *after functioning we satisfy
the authorities with avant survival on foreign funds, sources
and performances from Sabah, gravel bears, west synecdoche
encampments and Nuestra Señora Santa nearby everything,
comme on dit common human song and movement at a research
group*—those wooden stones set in devices formerly glued
by power, yes holy structures, veils, séances, labor handles
held up supple cant the edges of national reign fields, being
doubled and chopped in pieces, settled in a bowl with
frankincense, the dark encouragement sprouts up versions
of a sweet smoke wellspring shuttered here in the stone glass
ground spikes dug to turn the earth into a body you can
drink, *to convert*

lying down
others take off the millennial yoke, live like the person

playing the piano with stock feet in the memes, stand like
a comfortable photo modeling its won blind feeling, the
immaculate stylist with hats shaped like vulvar tufts and the
book won (she claimed) by Monsieur Blanc who was also
a model practice diamond cut for genial face crimes, *nous
sommes stoppés* he often said in responses, interviews with
loaded mouths that threatened to destroy the metonymy he
lived by and that she'd up till now, up till today not failed to
answer;

it's all in the letter, no longer rushing by ghost pilot spirituals
trembling in the front curling their stony hands inward; in
this sense she was born at the right time for her defections,
back to get some sleep she lay further down in the bed by the
window, giving herself again to love trembling discipline like
the question looking for an alphabet of the body that does
not exist;

in a prescient answer he had sent the notice and his export
pamphlets on a crystal boat, his exports went to earlier cloud
banks *okay, okay, his experts all went to a deeply posited series
of united countries* to report back in a series of psychological
dictions long-suffering sapless vivid habitations destined for
Ngana Nui ngana roa—your performance is a chorus on the

pier toward interior disassembly, as far as the country went for a show-down *Ngana Nui ngana roa:* "to the audience our work became extreme into the unknown," the actant donning the mask, wanting to know Hiku-leo who put it on our heads so slowly we didn't notice the honorific names

and a factotum, like an act of repairs we read your book and we were exercised, Hotu wai ariki standing up to open the hubristic laboratory background *where feverish alchemists of meaning* hung from books, dragged along like back in the days declared absent from felicity, from the western funeral where she lay with her head thrown back on the box where you were, the initiate dead in the kitchen, *al que quiere* working on dependent metropoli and preparing, preparing to evade the core sample thrown into her head from in between

that human planet moving recourse through a prayer for amnesia made to a you-itself: she had felt it on the other side of the initial summons, the para-innocent beginning accident that could not be deferred: a letter half-addressed

hovering
on it, in it, hovering your arms pained your legs as though pinned to un lit fait de miroirs *furniture made out of the deep*

ground in between though it's construed as far away, dug
into knowing and not knowing what can absorb the graft
of shared subjecthood: the furniture is breathing the crystal
doorknob glows the suitcase waits *the trip is going forward as
planned,* the travel hooks itself to the apparatus of answering
wet recurrent textual cords working around the question
dropped into the day *he said anything could happen,* a bird
immediately crashing into the window

appealed its verisimilitude, impetuous one—*now as we are
leaving I can say many friends and agreements are ahead,* the
opportunists uncover serious grimaces breaking out in his-
tory's striped tents though *they naturally began to ask about it*
the gold-bathed rush victims are far from your lettered bless-
ings (oh honorific sire she grimaced) we are far away cha-
grined and purposeful, *I was there yes I took part* sitting in the
chair at their representative chambers joining the showing
Tiki Te Pou-Roto with its Ambered and Imbued self-prom-
ises, large numbers of the regenerative visitable; we were up
on the heights calling Bluff to each other over the story water
ground river town

and my sisters, my sisters said benedicta tu in mulieribus you
are your own womb mouths given ex omnibus, we have made
our vellum from the dispatched extroversion of that grace

with such stationery she'd writ before until they *said we don't want or need to make people happy and* took the claimant by the hand, opening the cloth wrapped around her interior state, while someone at the other end took hold and pulled until the person spun into a garland as if willingly possessed haere ake tenei, to ake te papa ki te whare

near the waterfront our own conflict images working plastic rifles, their clothes thinned during a life in masks, Tahiti Iti walking and the coat being laid over brush strokes of shadow sitting that day without escape, notable resemblances of forty people or forty thousand sitting on a divan ground dug up and very like a mufraj holding outlines: a red circle meeting place where a police drone ends up chanting invocations by the now-quiet plastic rifle and a cancelled juridical revelry plays out (again) its testament for this soi-disant

valiant in her cloths, her meat fright dressing and undress-ing, she slips back borrowed from similarly baited paths near Whatitiri's invented meetings held without forcing history to be made in a building that shoots arrows into itself, aiming at a blood-myth for secrets surrounded by highlights: a per-son calling "you" can be thus prised, killed gently at begin-

ning and end, then called up from the dead to mimic the
spiritual war *for example when you practiced to be human you
were sitting with your face hidden by shadows looking like birth
mark soldiery in the heights, symbols run right through her chest
you can never say it only once,* the sentence pronounced gives
birth to its own repeating echo rifling across that room then
ringing *where there actually aren't ever enough books to read*

she sits up smoothly at the ringing phone then hovers breath-
ing and finally moving her mouth in a position of smiling *as
they were sitting in shifting numbers* partly

from the mental architecture crammed in events slammed
into the filaments of the waiting door, all this spiritual wood,
your own torso being bent toward the wealth estate, knowing
of who . . . of the eighth day crowd, when you slip-form the
map and apprehend half-like that you quomodo accipt

negativity bewildered and attraction on your face inveigled
in this adumbration of eternity spelt as dead, your reaching
hands dove first . . . alun et doubles doucement pressés my
sisters, my sisters, your ears fold out your mirrored torso
blanks, the inside's insides nearly spiritual ceramic (at last)
the deal you make to live externalized, bones worn on the

outside sheered from holy fascicles close between you and
the Culminant Soul shivering underneath a coat of chants,
the engine of your skin holds the still sound in the stone
phone—echoes *it is true* knowing as belief's an indeterminate
breath out as you listen under the wide waters, your throat
swallowing your eyes stinging a little against the aft light . . .
while her ears pray to open to the outside sounds of vehicles,
the clack of soft tree branches, rush of air that *shift* of conti-
nuity underneath her warrant wokeness retenus, he had then
in that court room been trying to say *there is time or there is
motion equivalent to time* as you were

driving through the war zone on your first time out the poly-
urethane operating theatres floating at levels near the caravan,
they were operating on large bodies you were telling to the
corner of your eyes you stared ahead and watched the Rep-
resentative throw an offspring very far, very far toward the
large body of water that was the edge of the conflict's arena,
the soft bridge having been smashed along the middle and
its pieces dangling wooden half-way across the appearance
of sky; and did the offspring live, was it live already thrown
symbolic breathless; did it raise some other rémouleur bri-
gade, did the caravan have any plan to stop or was it doing
your tour, apostasy of shared agreement tearing something
out inside your body

putting on the clothes that took her entirely from a sense of
warmth or heat—*filmic scenes repeating warmly ki i tēnei wā*
playing inside the textual brain its throngs the caravan like the
close room tuning up, the green land brown dirt practicing
at the edge of the brain now where the beloved community is
looking for answers or equation, what links them to the ques-
tion coming onsite with

the visitor
keeping your jaw in place, your answering voice taking you soon
where the hampers hold parts of your body until they assemble
again—your brain, your heart, your memory pressed together
your mouth pressed in your face, stella hau, the domino effect of
interior projection cracking mynde cloth, the mao-mao of the
petite soeur, je n'ai rien entendu the suitcase fondling yet our
conversation is fallen from love into nothingness without
which nothingness she cannot be

close to Higher Experience, at the very door; the anatomy
of the room is a mystical tideline, my sisters, an enactment
of Aura nurturing a non-missing place people talk about as
though it isn't there, the susurration of a sprung resolution
among the given and your works in dim harmonics, with
really tiny pictures of delicious wafers on the side table,
stolen and re-consecrate fondled absently by her fingers, the

sun shaft under which you stand for a moment some direction
turning, the sacred taxi that was there after you had walked,
oblivious, through its path, smashing your hand and getting ready
to tell a story that people hear familiarly "close to you," the faces
of apartments with outsides sheathed in civic rims—*she runs her
hand across her cheek delicate to the breath of air*—dim lights of earth
alulas turning in veridical direction

itself close by want of spreading out her hands on the cloth subdi-
vided by peonies, crocuses, cactus snails, a scene of arrested rushing,
the suitcase turned by giant ideas, the watery air shifting its sighs
inside a kenoary lino touching, tu es disponible having answered
the stone phone with a constant surprise whose mind

whose tongue, layering layering (plinth harpers ready to sing) the
back of the visitor getting sore and subdividing, the head fuller
and subdiving, the vehicle even now making a demasiado parecido
STAND UP AND WALK imperative for days alive, possessed like
a spiritual bar to answer, conscientious, slow, our inner castle—*are
you listening my sisters, nusquam hic* she says to lighten interior
passages, each fold again the map spread out inside the cranium
sparking its red stars, sorbing dewy ink on the stone phone adding
a response meant for your ears and my forgetting

evening

in the ulterior law, in the drinkable city her body swerves into a molt
some call spiritual androgyny, su muerte y las llegadas desperdiciadas
constituyen sólo una parte de la maquinaria de la continua, a shadow
realization y a hachazos, cortar y alterar: she's sitting on the bed a very
long time, see, wetness contained by permeating skin; regard her missives
painted on objects turn invisible (you can hear them roaring outside the
window, heaving the cart with promises alternately Germanic, wayside,
and solemn, lodestones font résonner des lieux) in the oncoming darkness
fondling her earthbound claims: *I took those bluestones to see how she
sees* and how they shine; *I threw knowing up for another habitation,* the
body's real disappearance engine for which quantities of earth infold;

her eyes turn further to the inverted sun inside her head until they're liquid
pools whose hot drapes quantify myriad fetters, one; one two three; one
two three four—internally on the lashes, the new blinks soft as korimako
kindly allocated from the then-living statue, whose ankles and touchstones,
foot occasionally feeling for the floor, glowing positions, are all a trial of
the version woman whose body's keyed in the correlative wires of this
building's replicas, themselves designed to double the inside of the
unwilled Act, *not really willed* stone faces having folded the outlined
decrees near where

the water falls out of her eyes and hits the floor like tiny seeds, accordion
breath sets her trembling as she imports a conduit of salivated thought
swallowed between speaking and listening, *talking with all of you* in the
specific place she's constant with the whakawhanaungatanga, sisters
conjured on the other side of the door's accumulating reverse-energy
collage, her longing truly a property of thirst and loops of magnetic divining
changed when *the instrument actually played neither of us fled*

a un cuerpo las propiedades de imán reserving the Embrace for stamped
Resemblance (we've seen that, sisters, she thinks then, how they mis-
attend the image covered in red thrown for the duration in places
simulcast with this one) *so you know excess can never be proven* in its
moment, events dripping with sentient food from temps cut naturally, an
invented belief suit required to palliate forces taking a blade to illustrate
practices regularly applied to supine genitals when cultures blood-mark the
child's body without consent, slicing across to anchor her to generalizations
that temper interest

for the animal waiting at the end of the room on which we shed light *we*
have detected as perspective, moving the body practices to give away
lightly though the Resembler provides new rationales aterrorizada de sus
trajes, stuffing newspaper and belladonnas, loops of film and invitations
that continue for days, announcements, banns, a daylog for approved
dialog, given to further bodies rolling as in a carpeteer selling magic out,
bright paisley stitched inside

an internally-lit soul plan in the form of a person whose tongue's stuck out
concentrating, coloring the fastidious pockets—blue, purple, green, red,
white epaulettes—for recurrence, listening to the voices of fine barkers
who create a kaitiakitanga of political economy, *you hear that* ink traveling
mandates a little bit lecteur, pero qu'est qu'on va faire quand your
ipukarea has been sluiced within perimeters *including you,* it isn't as
though your platform subdivides

the ground getting moderately soaked with her tears that plunge gradually
from where she is sitting down, down, down through the floorboards, the
cellar, the base stone, the aforementioned living ground *your feet push
through accidentally as you fumble the ambulance of knowledge before the
vocative body's spring,* as though observation is a kind of cruelty willing to
centralize above waves of paper whose lineaments are too quiet; they
ripple; oui petite soeur, je comprends tout because the body blazons, and
when that deed shall be done and how it shall be done is unknown

amidst the red tears given she would swear by Mary rooms,
in the wished-for shape of that woman's soul, a form of persuasion
apparitioning its objects:

improvident, as in causing the curtain to slice through change communally,
a rushing backward finally explicit to the cloth
dress coming on to the floor

letting me out at last, tiny power to confound the suppliant, to box the
mind in wraps made from her korowai, feathers changing fully from
familiars, riffling their transformance spheres, spiritual acrostics *j'ai visité
without permission (n'hésite pas) except that given by* coming near

when the barker calls (her erstwhile medium flexible cohort vanguard) on
statues bought with national shields—*we can place our anonymity right in
with the solitude of others,* while the Republic strangles itself with a fine
long-handed-down luxurious scarf *for a replacement in worldly satisfaction,
like if you can't quite breathe in the struggle then you don't really Need, do you,
your suitcase full of meat being the thing you suck on when you're hungry,
your own fingers doing the trick with the lock when there's a heat in your
brain or your tensegrity keeps you wondering what it feels like to be* Jesuitical,
really, or like the saline woman accesses the cleanliness you admire while
layers of contingent pretense stiffen all your flesh—you can see:
such a one has never starved, never talked fondly about meals she's had,
enumerating their qualities as a substitute (*suck on the suitcase, keep the
meat nearby*), the cutlery arranged on that table whose distance is
insurmountable from where she lies still, an expectorable difference flat by
her investigated hands—

*I'm sorry I held your head that way, little animal, lithe animus whose
cartographic simulation still suspends* the muscles easing statue's sleep,

your cellular affection a stochastic of false positives—as long as the
present circles arrival, leaves flutter, distant unsettlings of ground, while
her ectopic breathing focuses the people underneath the building having it
out, holding sound as light inside the growing darkness ground, making
their say in sharp memory echoes emanating in the room, her skirt hitched
up for the spiritual water to be avoided now at all costs, batted back
parere in the cloudy ground arranged inside her chest, imprisoning
reality's non-ideas; held on the plush seat the face shoots open in
astonishment at the plenitude of the breach mouth when morning's crack
gave way to spiritual water, to the legs entering the air breathing

in material culture, in the questions officially posed to her or will be posed
supposing the ripped light of day gives way to delivery, whether
the body of the letter will grow to form an oubliette large enough for
constraint, the wording iced into her cortex whose kinetic purple holds her
very still, does not replace bolting the cloth open with your teeth,
given to a wrenching mechanism you can suppose

before she is finished she takes a survey of all possible interpretations of
failure you can see—*it's all right, the room is a large animal and you a
portable cage inside it, being in another corner seeking a question with the
impatience innocent of life*—romping among the carpet grass to interpose
between her and the suitcase of meat, the books barking in a different
difficult language poised in the centrality of that spiritual kiss,
as though you really think "it will make a difference" if you
show up with the right bucket of meat for consumption's implements
the problem with you is you try too hard

the Representative points out again, over and over, a slow scape of the insides straight out the window of the shared vehicle, clean vomit and the slurred evening crawling along the balustrade of political apartments on your knees as you answer the examining with the whole movement of your body broken at just the right place her mind blinks in the middle of an imaginary sacred that does not resemble an answer, her fingertips suctioned into the oath until the tips break open bleeding into surfaces *the need-for-bandages your falling apart ears fraught with the phone streaming,* her hair pulled straight out against the pillow each strand blown off course toward

the authority clearing its throat in the line of tables at the chamber late at night where she sat with script-curved shoulders imagining the eternal present as though it were a future made of stone de este momento de esplendor

resulta una obra anónima, her casa marking that well: the double sacristy private (chamber of the lettrified heart), the shuttered windows filtering the past entirely through her anatomy, parceled in the letter bargains with absent persons you miss, *you miss . . . come along here and sing to me of a time whose instruments replace me with your own tears for a while,* inside the egg that Lady Belief has brought today

without apology, as there is no one to pardon, the sky increasingly broken
from its perch, river towns and platelets filling up her inside like dirt
streams . . . *essaie encore dans la bouche écho essaie encore* speak for the
level, try to get up . . . say hello to the combination of bones and cartilage
and muscles and movement la bas et entiere *say hello* that make up the
uneasy anatomy of your circumference, sin manos sin pies en la tierra, sino
la tuya, she has slowly moved back up into a sitting position from hours of
the lit lamp, a look like a hundred years *as you sit, say hello to the curve of
the interior room,* where she had a more heartfelt sorrow and a more
grievous desire like we mean it again for real this time, your bright stream
turangawaewae the held thing you want to take out and explain
"intellectually" to the warm wooden heart inside the suitcase

in the warm dirt where the body islands itself with weather animus or
strange, isolated pharynx like people diving or erupting in relation, people
startled by reaching the slow curve eventual crux then, little by slow . . .
shift by deal . . . giving over to the next dry wave of air's electrolytes . . . the
tassels and reaping find you in the house apartment room cell in which
you're given the sprung cart, or the horse you've pushed, your definition
rider tantamount to relics the woman with the suitcase full of meat
pantomimes as rituals of possession, such as walks on the riverside spirits
well in hand convinced by the diadems of that body trailing you or sniffing
ahead, the river long and some less neutral color on which floating
stamens hover blue, obtrude the glass, scintillant scotoma
an image of friendly death right next to that memory of walking *you know
the drill,* the occasional visit or harmonics or the walled disposition of that,

waking up there after a darkness of non-possession, walking on the edge
and calving fatalistic troubadours, the shades walk by you filling the
atmosphere as dead and live as ever, your own shade half-created, half-
measured and it is very gentle; the more we have it the less we feel it, all the
breathers who have stood there sifting ions through a wet iconicity of dirt,

covering visions of loving the other's water extended along the surface
infusing large and fast below, as when talking to someone on the black and
white floor, squirming on the tiles *one told her only afterward* feeling like
this lesson repeats the diadem, the statue's expression ah extendit folium
tersum, the witness bosoms heaving entangled hair across their visibility
you are following in a much other time when you see the woman
approaching with her suitcase full of meat, she's like a banshee or a
boatee, someone you can't recognize though that's all right because she's
regardless *ad excitandam legentis mentem,* the population wedged there
next exceeding fine as they are, determined anyway, the lacerations on the
surface eyes what you see, what you say hello to

as she surprisingly walks up and asks you something, you look like
someone who might know or who certainly does the answer to her
question, the boulders that tumble between skins *the answer to equations
people riding, many tiny people riding equations over your body with
certitude,* they are going to tell you what they've learned to declare—
that's why the headache feels familiar, these are aspects of the expression
close enough to love that defines where a fable betrays itself: tes mains

partout dans tes pensées *banshee, banshee,* she shakes her hand in your
face with her gentle frustration to move, she holds her suitcase and
pictures of her palm dress covered with hands that wove, her hair dress,
her dress of white tears, her dress made of word-stripped pages the tāniko
bands doing duty around her arms, the photo-image she carries in her
caravan, her eyes cut tourmaline in the head, mouth sucking on breadfruit
with teeth perched in the gaze, her arms holding the suitcase still while she
stops unseeing, mujer sola

although I urge you to forget everything but the blind awareness of your
naked being, you close your mouth *in the steamed-in car Replica agreeing
things are symbolic and allegorical,* the streaming lights from the building
show the Slicks being all Fine and Good as it goes, so long as you can fill
your lungs with a deep cloud and blow it out, hugely, blowing to increase
absence, blowing the Slicks away,

deep breathing in the known while the Cloud roars through . . . with no
considerate strength in its noise it bodes terminals pointed toward new
imperialisms, ceaseless regenerates, relics renew . . . as you look, peeling
from your face, the thunder is gentler, its moundy feet working along the
mountains walking, walking, the cloud an imperium of order pays proving
the grounds, walking, their lives tangible cavorting *not there as not here*
perilously close to faces streaming for the known . . . the mouths talk even
as the cloud opens close by the window, cavort, she pushes it open to
listen and the mouths get louder and smaller by turns, walking, walking
below, atlases stroking each other's virtues *if you know what I mean*

in time with the delivery of an animal to the
fold as experience . . . the cloud having no purchase either . . .
multiplying mana manna stone seas foresworn violet ultimately
duodecimal and, for you, oblivious

in the instrument keyed to her vocalics planting a deep tune in the outer
brain, seeping into the folds with tangential automatisms; as she stands
near, the curtains are very patient in relation with their windows, very
patient, the roof passive to the cloud intones "rain on me, shine on me,
open and close your faces with the patience of the convert" who can do
little not associated with heretical adoption; the hands in the face again
putative authentic until you can see where the inside of the skin meets its
underlife, the vitriolic subtended, warrants issued for parts of her body
repeating—"you have a well, very deep, you draw from"; come closer and
tell me "is that a dress or is it evidence"—

like a sieve world the sterynges come nearer and nearer, swirling down
from the cloud in a pattern of aerated water en la cama por analogía y la
caída de un techo de soñadores atonal buscando el pelo de las runas, the
rhetoric from conventional life telling her off again, giving her the goods
they bore; rain wheels push down on the cloud in patterns of ramp, her
skin becoming like cloud pressed through the windows on the roof,
pressed and not willing or but ramparts, folding, curtains, edges, paper
ends, window panes stacked against the inside of the building where she

waits, in her dress with the tissue wrapped around so her skin's burned cold *like holding on the bridle of an animal who does not want to be held you get burned then though not with fire, paper flowers porting the ink having had time to dry by way of a translative sport, brought through tunnels where they can no longer breathe so their labels descend under glass, chlorophyll arms bent through agreement like the colding apartment where they breathed in that moment,* the cloudsign of your breath as you walk near the door understanding the continuity of her carven representative heart, a trafficked avenue of ghosts depending

night

nearby, closing the window, rippling without detection for the circulating
bodies held in by the trappings of warm furniture; her eyes turn to curl
around the book profoundly available to view, street sounds in the mouth
as bodies mask their torsos, the surge inside torsos hover very near warm
letters whose chemicals couple at the ready; invisible events flare
occurrence like when Someone tells you how to coax relations in the
tremolo *thanks for that:* the head inside the tense bounty of the stone's
hot flesh beneath, an entire hot planet translate like that soul-body shift
configured for the feet kissing the ground (which she has done, moved
among Stations, blossoms tithed to this sole cleanse)

nearby, the ink on the cloth paper seeps for a milliner who wants to show
you (is ecstatic about its turns and demos) how to get there in your cloche
d'eau, white-green or saved is the water from washing the linen swirling
down the disappearing drain, *she follows it as in a miracle play, the medial
darkness smocking around the gentle cloth wrinkles as you open toward
the drain tunnel with ideas leaning in to keep you company, holding your
bids while you grope with the other hand critical acoustics, listening for the
next bend where the cloth pushed through, the body's blood pipes dangling*

inside tensed like a matrix pretending for grave reasons it's a stump or a misdirection in the biospheres

nearby, staring like a Mary procreating her own self, the number of loops make it fairly certain identity would come back, the wood standing for her insertion into *some kind of Barque making way for her performance* organ music in the cambium where you press your ear to the bark and can hear it, the wooden car coming through the claustrum where she's standing with her suitcase waiting (paper mouths intoning vibrato in the silo, on the braided sheets, in the joinery, in the blacksmith shop by the table with berries on top, on the vehicle in the sand where wintry trees grow remembering the barrier between life and Other Life, the parametric body hovering its allowances),

moving among the documents in an outward-tending array of vehicles starting with the if, temporis exacte servabit amorem moving toward the hunger of the limbs, saturated with the crystal subvention we read about over and over, sisters wandering through the castle breadth whose interior gardens stroll themselves along over and over, their bodies becoming cloth, the earth moving with its self-recognized waves as strong letters contrariing unto the clean hid sight

walking the earth was like those waves but so slowly we could not normally feel; in the interior garden of the symbolic dream there were komodos who could fly, they flew up and the ruffles of their throats expanded as they reached the height of the tall thin trees bearing the fruit they most desired, so the woman flying to void awey all the outward parts of that wode—at a lower altitude she could only admire and be proche, the Power talking on the stone phone invivid, turned on the line depth multiply il s'est mis dans sa bande passante where *his scars will subdivide*

the bandwidth she found that moment when she lost her present suitcase and now with only her clothes and streaming *the only place I saw her occupy the deep stitches of the clothes, scarves, hairpins, explicative hats,* dimensionally peculiar substances around which the group would hover fingers extruding from their eyes, a closer look urgido por la necesidad el jardín busca el miedo el balido tipo el ojo del cielo the length of it dentro de la brillante tierra, her scarves falling continuously around the water take thes cryingys fro me and lat me havyn hem be myself alone pressed to smelt like watery syllables

now colluded with the winds traveling manifests; inside the solid kotahitanga air voices call, the cloud grows larger and larger *inside you there's a commission,* an inquiry to feed itself akin to sutured Granada, a cession or cessation with which cultural genes whelm syllables in their tongues; unable to direct each other they become new, en el presente puede contemplarse una serie de elementos *though the will was not consulted we're already there,* the agglomeration of hybrid identities is

completely in that dirt digging through what was not so very long ago;
you've got joyance on your fingers, a whole cusp of selves subtended
in the new:
> it will have to cascade, to be that river by the highway
> you're assured is made of water coming from inside
> the earth around in fountainettes it circulates, it regurgles
> *like all fluid you feel is really blood* streamed with its identical
in a wash or wadi,

touching it gently in the Square your tongue comes out and licks
> *it tastes like salt and honey at once metallic and sensational*
in the well-used mirror waters, the dew on the windowsill she transfers to
her mouth to inspect, the dust hums on her tongue of viages and abood
holding onto the surface to keep from collapsing underground the
judgment scene, *the consultation going forward in multiple places*
magnetizing the inner building with that taste—her stone heft
at the ready, like a kind soul might take a portioned wāhi tapu and
thread it out to see the inside of her body slow unspooled manawa—look
here, have a look,
> *there you are in the middle of the Skype session looking*
> *Fabulous really honey it's a Look I haven't seen on you in*
> *years, an expression reminiscent of your future self no really*
> *I think the take is coming the midnight coffee is on the way*
> *the letter burns itself for eagerness we're all glad*
> *to experience the exchange we've been dreaming*
> *like for centuries now here it is and aren't you glad*

you're live for it—
giving way to a super-added time machine, a clean person meeting another
clean person whan sche sey hym comyn inside beneficent livelihoods,
strained with that pronouncement that we are "free in the now" and
what's good not to like

in such a chance, appetite itself respiring con un manto de seda amarilla
incrustada de perlas, the ground birds singing kū kū like sky birds in tune or
out of tune, the ones declared sentimental by substrate power ("god how
nineteenth century is that" you ask your teina, in the alien priory sisters
speaking to each other with invisible others standing behind their screen
faces pouring in at once, looking as though three dimensional copy
machines voluptuate and there you are) in accord with incantations flashed
all day out the other side

she reaches in and fondles the words on the tongue,
wraps the room in which she venerates   engagée avec
        un coeur les enchantements   d'esprit c'etait comme
j'irais à la place où tu penses the shift from one posture to difrens
one's arc du corps encore planchant   sur les nuages believers
amazed as though visibility were a purchase on area
glass modules propping up the eye que pasaba muy cerca de
ellos keeping company as the words hemistitch one sidereal
        frame to another on your stretch-sail adoring

the sound of the leaves (pressed together now that Love responds to
Reason's questions), *the clean screen of your skin a vanishing overlay*

children earlier nearby yelling and exuberating *hit-troooo,*
adolescent trees showing off, mini cars strutting their instruction
night light windows straining under the sights
they carry: atolls whose subscriptions lapse whose rings
drink deep les yeux de la planète so fully they achieve *an outward and*
visible sign everywhere archeology could wish
pushing up under the crust of the earth glowing
innard's spirit conditionals ready to meet in the wolde of this apartment
whose progenitors lavished the exterior with licking tongues by way of a
paint job—*it takes a long time and you get splinters in your tongue and*
rough tiny pebbles drag along andgit blossoms splay a posse of refusal, you
fall off the roof

when you are almost done, hau . . . and your tongue throbs in disarray, en
la noche su reposo se cierra otra se abre the aptment exteriorized by the
contact with human licking *and who's gonna live there now with animality*
extruded all over the windows and tiny chemicals digesting through the
ceiling, *like a wash coming for you in the sentence* as she sits there calm
enduring the infrared light storms that invade her spheres, very like a
massing body full of dark and wet she is Traversed, spectrafied, inhabited
by possession's call (monic bird songs from outside pounding from
within, the constant electric fields of others amend her into a Variety of
Experience others feel might be a problem, a constitution not aligned

with dedicated streams of personality fielded by planetary light sound,
a storm whose wastes are further afield than calling, calling into her
their mild electric

range birds calling on grasses in trees, the weak timber expanding voice-
lined furnishings, the paranoid narcissist inhabiting infrared eyes at the
Somnolent Incapacity of the Real to reignite an expectation of holiness or
unitary fields) as in: who ever expected something other than joined ideas,
where does unalloyment fancy come from, the chamber elle-même
contient la constitution de ses images, chaque événement connu as
memory, chaque pensée un souvenir foretold by the consequence of
what's happening right now without her yet being able to remember,
insofar as thought is mirror war reality to the touch—

she shakes her head at the thought, vaya ideas tienes, sitting by the green
wall closed in her clothes, her legs held up her hand on the suitcase,
trembling getting readier the scraping sound of earth in the world
puckered and slowly, slowly, growing to a tremulous crustiness that breaks
through in the inferred storm, the clinking sounds of vocal chords donde
una puerta *the cold fingers around your clothes holding your limbs and
torso holding themselves as though you could hold your breath until you
died to live* dear Tantalus, dear l'autre liesse dear dark glass Lilium
candidum dear dear dancer, Implacable arrivalist, contamos con vuestra
presencia y apoyo para estos proyectos

all the way through until you reach your limbs like a suitcase, keeping the
caustic body reaching the trunk casual to your extremities, your sacky
heart closeted as it creeps up to your brain phenomenally (called as much
as we are virtues of surprise, cutting across the parish choices linked to
belief's exteriors, the building is amazing in its totally determined violence
she thinks like a sure heart surtout a telephone, carved in the wood the
birds nest past the constant haunting of non-telephonic
effects, la voix performing the loved being with a beauty of lacerate
inflections, sounds of birds or thermal noise
past the end of my ear, this waiting room a paradigm of the loved
telephone placed in a situation of pleased exhaustion, like the times you
know the conversation will go on only so long in the departure of the other
scribing distance that in turn we know only as we know what closeness is,
each any number) waiting-not-waiting, constanting, the Sorrows of Wide-
Eyed Capital being-not-being any water like a purple cup entirely blessed
—like your own control of the body escapes, the scaffolding is permanent
to evade taxation that accrues at the finish, trends in those places where
the heart is beating openly in places where the roof is left off
and the walls maybe not complete, and the clothes over binding
in the body that would otherwise unfurl . . . funnily different from spiritual
debt collapse at the failure of your bodily capital (aforementioned) project,

in the room the telephone rings with love's imaginary put in place of prior
form, une voix altérée figured as a Mirror Wound seeing the other
overturned on the bench tucked into the "window area," dabbled from an
alien register . . . the tall figure who is very tired cocoons
une lettre ne lus setting out a dread graffiti's query of lingo,
a case of genitive departure *weighed around*

bidan like an idiosynthetic mechanism, the voice also necessarily imbues
the stone telephone she will have carried; it's funny because it bears a
total resemblance to earlier phones considered "real" that reach
somewhere, but *this* phone, this lode phone is simply heavy with her
weight in wairuatanga: each one pressed on glow for each other like runes
you're taught to read or learning new ones, places and accidents and
curlicues, veins and tropes and wires, floors legs walking, rain patterns,
wind, breath of others, the sound of fluid and its harking bodiment, the
taxonomy of skin as she touches it and look: the entered vehicle and its

rain sounds, the radio completing its programs with separate plans,
listening to this phone avec la voix d'un coeur lacérée avec cutting
tools for the wood of her tiered heart's very own sacristy, consisting of the
body parts she's spiritually cut from each therapeutic index: stone robes,
robes of temporal cloth   conducting whether via   une double
structure qui permet d'en faire la genèse the stick and tread wails in tiny
millions—la traduction full of fire drumming, the hands clicking and the
syncopation arriving at last the tick and attitude there it is, the person

calling without words and the interspersals of that load; it'll come up
chirping, the call replacing some kvetch or advertisement, such meat and
wailing in the arms as you wave them up and down in that future, your legs
up and down, walking the parcel she's learned her sisters look at the . . .
mind trees and how they're thinking as the cloud expands amond . . . . . call
out like that to abeyance, over quietude cells lingering in the wet half-shed
. . . . . . extiende una mano, conoce nuestras misiones, truisms so full as to
be envisible in the mouths of those you talk with who believe with *each
other where we are*

*the world's torso fatted with wet, a bridge built from one ear to the other,
the hands tied together with arms looped in a crazed circle, mondiale et
superfice, Gargantuan really, the result of a feeling that the cage is
bulksome, like being put inside your own suitcase and carrying yourself in
act if not execution without your own varieties of sacral experience
including interior song,* staring at the crystal door knob straitened in the
dark … amidst a field of perceptual cross-integration while on the move
across the room, *singing in tongues that cannot be heard, feeling the
planet crack and start to reel out as you held my hand beside the mortal
animal*—so called she looks up to hear
      herself reciting to a large airy room of listening judges,
    they were   listening and listing on their papers,
   the woman lived for several years off-screen and then
    came back, the representative Lover looking at her
     with a sanitary measure of possessed light, as the sentence
   goes, so the room goes with its curtained hover,

with great gulps of visual richness she led   across the arena of her
contemplating years during which time
        became a living painting with aberrancies   one could note
when very close, when really looking, her in-dwelling eyes knotted with a
fixity of concentration, deinde vero prefatus cuing to enter

tiny fate whose crystal shores trip overlap, ou tenons nostre estat
her limbs were disappearing with a deprived majesty, a florescence
individually examined by the arena full of listeners who had color, sound,
area, and reckoning to abide with, from lungs to the next word she sang
arcs across the neutral cloth, hoping for compurgation
maybe not even personal whakawhanaungatanga *maybe not even*
that but oh god her breasts moving in the fabric because she hasn't learned
to cover herself internally against anyone binding flowers on her training:
        to build the cases in which she self-presents is a worry
            or a bother, then sharp readiness shred magnet
        flits around from glass the lenses of your skin cloud
        cover not unveiling habiliments continually ago

nor were the colors accompaniment or measure, they were instead her
idea of how she had moved during that interval—the night birds clacking
the air—that was the arc we lived in without permanent questioning,
holding our Giant Flesh, holding our anchors to weigh up the floor, the

starry reach of the ceiling lights, the velvet cloak pads some called
whippoorwill the wallpaper sang, some called ambulatory the chairs called
out, their buttocks languorous for mercy and their tongues held soft inside
their still mouths not speaking, lips pursed for relation, not background nor
even foreground but a middle place where

she waltzed right in, *smooth as you like,* as they open their residual mouths
a realization when she turned slowly there were trees, and the sound of
the whippoorwill had been coming in mobile strobes, the torso clenching
ready to rise the tongue separating from the roof of the mouth to speak,
rising as smooth as you like where the clouds begin to shake her like a
violet in the strata between ascending, another vision ymaginem et
similitudinem suam getting close, accepting in the torso of her heart the
claimant of her lays, her vast investiture what happens

when we enter into darkness beyond understanding finding not only a
growing lack of words but a weird resistance in what
we say to the postulates of culture: come in and assemble your ideas
slowly give or forgive yourself
                    hey, it's a nightly event, in a moment strewn across the

mystery our eyelids slowly weightening, whitening, breathing the cloud into
our lungs to match the aureoles singing, the fingers when you hold them
out for Someone you don't know to tremble slightly devised as a shake of
hands, a trembling of hands, a smile in perigee to earth as super-version
swilling with additives, the possible sequential bodily look round
for the modulated tones of what became then suddenly a loud voice—"a
life sentence for heresy against the ideology of authenticity"—smiling,
that is at fruit-smelt or idea food, the legs slowly
shunning their abbreviates . . . come what may you can see what the
temperature has brought along: chill, vulperism, habituated lithe
verticality, the crossed eyes this time the people who look at your traveling
clothes and cannot place themselves across receding orisons of their unwill
and *that's okay, the situation understands itself, the table of food you're
walking toward with idea clothes as in I think I love this place I think it's the
place for me, the name's a trochaic skipping vowel bubble, a staccato
riparian fillip accrued to micro-instruments, metonymy on the ground the
feet you step they tinily abide your lids rose in the spiracles of the name* the
reappearance of familiar colors standing in for

a less temperate division of the climacus resupinus, the animal boot
and tongue modes, the village floor plans as fires sweep their named
avenues where illuminated event ghosts sound baritone, begin to test and
true the tempering fidelity, *the full meaning of this marvelous illustration* a
simple fire across the mouth cut gently with opening as they wait eremitic
a few more minutes for people to come *vocalize;*

we must be patient; the land is very far away and bodies can float only so
fast after all, the mild enjambment of who really stood in the breach
scribbling its familiar too whoop thtooo lhloooo
vivisection finds itself in middle living swoons itself *too whoo* in gentle
swells itself *pouri pouri* stirring
night birds bidding a chance to see, swells and waves
across the path all orbital streaming toward a redoubtable sleep happening
for others, blithe truistic parenchyma event
as made to order   now *what you do Sweet fixate, you have a draw or*
Fixate, the lumps of sugar made to offer, the milk repelled, *show me how*
you drink it, how she finds the filial temperature show up and up, show up,
hotter and hotter

as the messenger does its stuff, her feet swollen with listening to one
person after another say things she believed or thought were true, or at
least true to someone's experience, in wittenesse of whiche thinges
anyway having some ground in the actual *come to find out,* come to find
out el domador knew no better nor is a medial ideology any gentler, lives
holding the bent cup proportioned to the scala penetrometer
sunk directly to the skin, *knew all that,* she knew all that as
the animal cries at the zoon logos far down the street from this room, its
rights and substances completely extruded to a hierarchy not involving its
ultimate needs though certainly its average ones, its dictates of medial
okayness all spoken for —

okay okay, the name imbues the stone on which she sets her cup of tea
and *this is how you shall know* breathe in and out, breathe it
bare, deserted, lovely, wild: ki te mea ka tatanga te wahine
ki te mate, a kahore te ariki ki reira
she knows the substance will come through whether or not the letter is
worded carefully, the advent will do what it knows,
sightful and clenched, the torso heavy though nicely turned inside its
clothing, the fabric doing its utmost, happy cloths walking the legs, happy
screening tea givers with braided hair gone scary-cat,
street show putting up its smiles beloved
strewn across the screed one so adamantly caresses as one walks, future
time being the causality spread across *she thinks she knows something at
last* her face has a map engraved in it, that's what it is, read the map, use
your topo-symbology-grid set it bottom side down

pacing the change hub like a sieve, je vais t'écrire quand même, ton visage
voyant dans le ciel les yeux si broken whence
the shards of warm light bathe me, illuminate envers ton esprit avec lequel
la femme danse dans ses mains, une sorte de
clay of wet wool moist and pliant the warm brain open in the hands she
smears across her belly gathering, gathering, the pliant shift
and her vegetal exuberance worked in the cloud
upending the totally innocent time of made desire, "je vais t'écrire dans la
chambre humide" bringing the result to you directly dousing and densing
for true, wiggling for the want of

verrei have you clenched that, *can you get up,* is the cornerstone fallen directly on you or only sideways like so it's "done" or "everybody is" crawling across the doctrine, *do you need help* or can we hurry

divided, une attention à l'autre à tout moment the trees so familiar you can see the sprouts gradually unleafing, unfurling, the granules of the tiny bloated green veins turn finitesimally

each hour the dark sun moves its spirit unseen *i te kaha o te mahana: you are speech gathered; conveyed and made lacewing trace;* the sound box moving in time to novel coups, a full new brand never seen so clearly to *find your locative belief chain prayer beads, super-icons dangling a Lost Horizon* rentré dans la grande paix paternelle: the Real Life fish painter turned around to be artificial and tropic;
she drew then images by a babbling brook fed by a waterfall where the mists are hidden from culminance by an imploding fortress of os—

    stoppé droit (she's shaking with ink and discerns a collection of people evoking Pregnant Moments, estaremos preguntando the Central Fears of meaning programs and their literate dialog erat inanis
              in terms of eunic racked margins, jam in the ballistics
              problematizing the clarities of neo-trauma, a PR piece
                  of cake or toast, a PR thematized cereal pathos
              playing in the dark in modern terms) *what is really on the rational mind* what does it look like in front of the glass when no one is around, when plighted imaginaries flatten when you're pancaked in that *se retourne pour partir* swerve

she's studying in the dark the object
holding in her hand, having picked it up opposite
the apartment's defended position, the resident of a shadow
hovering in the accident; there's a salve of imperatives refoulant
de plus en plus proche from rubbing the paper in the ample dark like
postmodum verodic prima mensis scratched into
some pretty raw satire obscure as DNA showing up
on the pin, a superfice of identity birds buzzing with soul, reversing the
expedition, turning the cold tables toward your legs
offering exegetical continuities—*note: need to investigate blood writing as*
directed escape from faith's revisionary arc—increased by
a page no one's ever seen, photos that never existed, whose referents are
ready to meet the door fueled by flares shooting over the head
disappearing behind a fantasy of the republic yearning toward the
biodome, an extruded flattening of the body pushed into the phone whose
static energies are focused in a start, des gestes instrumentaux prenant
appui sur ses propres vides when we know there is no "music" we can
listen stripped of ears

for the wakeup call, listening for the steps to take,
calling with a phone inside the brain
for good and all imagined judgment embrace of evident time
never really going back to the body

still waiting at the bloody spot living on wattage
near a door, waiting for the end of night, her body replaced by stars

stone languor scarcely conscious in the private or personal, *still
ontologically out of place and inescapably countrified from the real grey
slopes with their green vertebrae catching the clouds, the pressing cloud
blankets euphonic surface shadowed really one could wonder, one could
slam against the said
exquisite new prayer writ from meeting in the witness*
        her tongue placed below the drop that forms at night, gentle
slow accumulation coming at phenomena, cooing over the obedient
scriptural art of time or okay
blessing the tangi's obvious trawl with red, the sounds of the sisters up to
date with mind also used to coax the bells to make correctness patient,
given over to some terms she was saving for the arc across which a body
can carry *in* and *of within* against and *for*—which, sentenced to a mouth
to get the distillation, la cassation est donnée comme serenade, it becomes
the *something which* the convergence of orality and gaze really do what
we agree to, dancing by
tara subduction couerhid and ouerlappid with innumerable substances

she had a shrinking morning economy approaching her idolatries, los
halagos de la imaginación hacen de este un libro sobre una mujer

arrodillada en la cama, the nude Sabbath slaking las nubes de la sabiduría fuera de la ventana raspando como las alas de aves en el cristal . . . perhaps the answer is not an answer at all but kerning stronge letters contrarying their own self-intercept; a battlement game immolation; the person coming out of mural ashes and getting round to the work of anyone's holy city, through which—as it feeds out forward of relation's mutual unfurlment—she walks with the nature of the conscious

meeting houses, little shops proceeding ahistorically, not fully spelled or borne of *not to mention contemporary meaning* asbestos peeled through judgment, fibre bleeding the red sounds infusing the hungry stone city victim hoaxing next to her as she walked then putting things into the suitcase, the big concert a kind of hoedown, assiduous formality of her courtside speech accepting hearsay heresy: the name in the forgotten text is Cleverback, diem ac noctem cordium *he rolls now because his body's missing the mean of happiness, the amputational precious belief* of the moral tide, persons of correctness ethicized fresh and indeed grossly heritage-oriented nothing put in her mouth can change her now very much as . . . . . . she's resolute in her posture, not altogether strange . . . dobbed in by mnemonic perestroika, Centro Histórico eyes fixed pero yo no soy lo que debes encontrar . . . and yet she fit that day in the star collision, ropes around her propositional chair plus proche:

assume a door, each window pane gives truck to a predisposed room into
which visitors come and go for reasonable bodies
flock boudin red foldingly aware of consumption's plan
in their matter, nothing planned but the tables and tables of edibles (they
are meant to discover, the vehicles stretch out formidably protecting an
imagined consequence es atreverse a viajar keeping the flora at bay), the
window sisters errant voluble, the song
agreeing to wait in a photograph proof minutes away, a trek across favor
for the letter standing arch-backed asserting a technical problem with
contact, the high green double bar flaunting
circles, eyes gently sprouted from that conventional Dictaphone qui
habitait the tube wound round her hair its spiritual rhizomes
being at not so much a Lower Level as placed in the Strangely Familiar, the
surface having grown warmer by the day wherein

       the woman is waiting with her head put under the position where
the drop of water will soon release
its dolomite calm . . . it's inconsolable in the bread of the soft ground,
the glowing identities of ilemite sands exchange
accumulation of the water, the woman's mouth waiting for
cultural perfusion *once answered here once we go straight, once we go*
with a slow discomfort almost as soon as the reaction—this *nothing*
undergone nowhere as she taught Love something she could not see clearly
in her reason by understanding's busheled light nor in the animal
glow yet feel truly emoticons struck in the sweetness of ink's blood
brought to its knees—

dont on a fini dans le quotidien par pure manque de conscience, watching
her own output over such longing, she took a half-drop told the god head
clearly touched hovering behind the percipient boot under whose aegis she
lies, reaching to sop the seal with several versions of
Prescient Precursor raided on that bench switching literacy both ways—
really wildly enthusiastic divergence from its future who stands and waits
there on a plane representing a mountain una vertiente tearing
l'esprit from security paradigms broached along the furniture here
symbolic to place a mastery (flying over the green land of hearts, a re-wirer
of anonymous desire frothing at the gob, consequential to a series of
mad men who nevertheless gain position in a leap we are endlessly
lurched in a great stage of established thinking
exaggerated mistressness to inward sight
both una astilla de la cruz and her suitcase an béal bocht the diaphragm
swallowed as an aphorism building a ladder toward a different see)
further from her whakapākehātia, inviting an acid pattern to affect
the Earth's Anterior extremely posited "point of view," a pinnacle
irritation kind of mystery intern singing herself naked, a contemplative
subsidiary of her body's trope;

her throat's dislodged from progenitive cloth at last
a bluestone set of eyeholes left disturbed during a consumptive period
about archives and a great revisitation where she waited (again) for the
wings to come move the alula of this landspit

in retrospect c'est la mise en évidence de cette double altération it's much
the same, tailing on your shoulders always pressing into their minds *I
couldn't disagree, I couldn't more array it,* an animated discipline fabric
on her lap's a mark of heritage embedded, he ao, he ao
the night sounds pushing into her now-solid ears congress for the faceless
inherited civility whose close creatures got nervous, rusty as a gate caked
at the bottom of the walk where anyone can hear it, one greater Love one
expert coming along, vous constatez que ces populations sont hic et nunc,
apatrides, roughly formed in words

te rakau ngakau crossed on recent salient capture (*spoke in a funk spoke
making the case, getting the name out*) korero also acknowledging
text and the face bent over a catapult problem a little too closely, not
bogged down in questions of
dig, dig deeper more like a touch she makes her breath in the stone room
next to the vent: il faut savoir qu'un mot c'est un nuage: tu l'enveloppes
quand tu l'approches en entrant; toute sagesse unflexing à la rencontre
to know in the individual, each word a node on the continuum that rises
without control, each word a body
who takes her hand looking on a walk across the room for the double-
chapeled one inside the other clear apartments with their softened door,
windows like eye-slits turned on a head lying down enthused new grunts
elective in our periods, *she are indebted to continuity* whereas
feminism and response, *go do go do* ad libitum
siting adaptation   standing up also coming along emotionally
by way of a walk across the floor cliff, holding queries holding questions,

an armful of questions spoken in return strokes
toward the doorknob crystal striding speaking to the diversified iron
identity, a rift foundation ready along
the door they're approaching from both sides.

textual note

The Long White Cloud of Unknowing invokes Aotearoa (land of the long white cloud), the Māori name for New Zealand, alongside the European mystical text *The Cloud of Unknowing* (c. 1375, anonymous). Additional texts provide sources and inspirations: *The Mirror of Simple Souls* (c. 1300) by Marguerite Porete; *The Interior Castle* (1550) by Teresa of Ávila; *The Booke of Margery Kempe* (c. 1432-36); Hildegard of Bingen's *Visions in Scivias* (1121-23) and elsewhere; *The Book of Privy Counsel* (c. 1375, anonymous); and Julian of Norwich's *Revelations of Divine Love* (1395).

I composed this book across several years and locations, starting in Spain and including Aotearoa, the UK, Canada, the US, and France. Many of the book's translingualisms were learned and invented during that time to perform aspects of the character's single day—itself an invention to explodingly compress multiples, including different Englishes and a devotion to the (punctuationally) single sentence. I think of this book as a poetic mystery: the sole character is the only one who knows what she doesn't know, for sure.

about the author

Lisa Samuels is the author of seventeen books of poetry, memoir, and prose—mostly poetry—including *Anti M* (Chax 2013), *Tender Girl* (Dusie 2015), *Symphony for Human Transport* (Shearsman 2017), *Foreign Native* (Black Radish 2018), and now this *Cloud* book. She also publishes essays and edited work, and sound and video work, and recently has been involved with visual art and with film (*Tomorrowland,* 2017, based on Lisa's 2009 book and directed by Wes Tank). Born in the US, Lisa has also lived in Sweden, Israel/Palestine, Yemen, Malaysia, Spain, and since 2006 in Aotearoa/New Zealand.

about chax

Founded in 1984 in Tucson, Arizona, Chax has published more than 240 books in a variety of formats, including hand printed letterpress books and chapbooks, hybrid chapbooks, book arts editions, and trade paperback editions such as the book you are holding. From August 2014 until July 2018 Chax Press resided in Victoria, Texas, where it was located in the University of Houston-Victoria Center for the Arts. Chax is a nonprofit 501(c)(3) organization which depends on support from various private funders, and, primarily, from individual donors and readers. In July 2018 Chax Press returned to Tucson, Arizona. Our current address is 1517 North Wilmot Road no. 264, Tucson, Arizona 85712-4410.
You can email us at *chaxpress@gmail.com.*

Recent books include *A Mere Rica,* by Linh Dinh, *Visible Instruments,* by Michael Kelleher, *What's the Title?,* by Serge Gavronsky, *Diesel Hand,* by Nico Vassilakis, *At Night on The Sun,* by Will Alexander, *The Hindrances of Householders,* by Jennifer Barlett, *Who Do With Words,* by Tracie Morris, *Mantis,* by David Dowker, *Rechelesse Pratticque,* by Karen Mac Cormack, *The Hero,* by Hélène Sanguinetti (transl. by Ann Cefola), *Since I Moved In,* by Trace Peterson, *For Instance,* By Eli Goldblatt, and *Towards a Menagerie,* by David Miller.

You may find CHAX at *https://chax.org/*